The Zombies Have Big Heads

And other observations from

The Freelance Retort

Unraveled - Vol. 1

By
Brian Moloney

ISBN- 978-0998733906
ISBN- 0998733903

Keymaker Publishing

Email: freelanceretort@gmail.com

Cover Design: Brian Moloney

Zombie image from ClipartKid.com

Also by Brian Moloney

The Kingdom of Keys
(Young Adult Fantasy/Adventure/Fiction)

The Little Red Christmas Ball
A story for kids and anyone whoever was...and would be again

Available thru all major on-line booksellers

Dedication

For Aunt Steve, my all-time favorite grown-up.

Gone, much too soon; you infected us with your "take no prisoner" laughter and made *everything* we did way more fun.

You told me I was funny...and I believed you.

Go figure....

"How we laughed...!"

Table of Contents

In the Beginning

This That and the Other Thing

First, let me say this is not a book about Zombies...at least not completely.

So if you're looking for a good old blood and gore horror story, I'm afraid you'll be disappointed.

Okay, sure...It has some Zombies in it, from time to time...but, really, what doesn't, these days?

My Zombies are more of the sociable, fun loving, neighborly variety than your run of the mill tear out your heart and eat your brains Zombies.

In fact, they live right across the street from me (long story but you can get the short version on page 13), so how could I exclude them from all of my skewed eyed tales of life....with or without the embellishments.

Besides, I can live without the neighborhood tension that would arise if they were to find out they weren't in it.

At least that's the plan....

I began "The Freelance Retort" in May of 2011 when, if you recall, the world was supposed to come to an end.

I figured, what the heck... it's a short term gig and folks might appreciate a little morning chuckle, while waiting for the apocalypse to arrive.

Well, as with most apocalypses, it didn't, so now I've been stuck writing these things for the last 6 years, once or twice a week...for the most part...usually...maybe.

It depends on the weather....

There's no real way to categorize what I write. In fact, most of the time I have no idea what it'll be until I start.

And a lot of the time I'm not even sure when I'm finished.

As you'll see.

I don't really have a genre.

Well, I did, once...but I lost it...I think at the beach when that odd looking seagull was going through my stuff.

I've written video scripts and commercials for

corporations...published a children's Christmas book, a young adult coming of age fantasy adventure and I've had a mysterious, metaphysical, humorous mainstream novel in the works for quite a few years that I hope to complete someday, if I can ever figure out what it's trying to tell me.

Which brings us back to this, "The Freelance Retort" of which I've compiled 600 plus told tales.

While I strive to be humorous in all, I like to think they run the gamut from silly to sentimental and insane to insightful.

I've tried to be judicious in my selections, choosing some of my early year retorting favorites.

Like I said, one never knows....

But I hope you enjoy them, just the same.

Brian Moloney

May 21st-The End of Days!

What Happens to the Nights?

In theory, I'm a freelance corporate writer, which means I

create everything from promotional, instructional, training videos to interactive on line presentations for various corporations and health care companies. In that sense, I guess you could say I'm a "professional writer" since I do get paid to write, work from home and have lots of free time to myself. However, most of my neighbors think I'm just goofing off.

In between mowing the lawn, raking leaves, shoveling snow...and did I mention counting sand on the beach....the stars sometime align, in just the right fashion, and someone from a small group of "regular clients" I've fooled into working with me through the years will pull my name out of a fish bowl and throw a project my way. This usually entails coming up with and executing a clever idea for a "Team" of executives who are promoting a new initiative or product, but who are basically trying to impress their peers and their bosses, so they can move up the ladder and assign this same task to the new "Team", next year.

I also have to put on pants...usually.

My wife, Z, is a nurse who's a cross between Florence Nightingale and Mother Theresa.

She saves lives.

I save the butts of mid-level executives.

Who do you think wakes up singing every morning?

But a peculiar thing happened the other day. I actually woke up feeling very upbeat and—dare I say it—"happy".

Borderline giddy, actually.

I even found myself humming. I was so stunned by this behavior I texted a friend who's familiar with my many, let's say, negative moods, informed her of the situation and inquired, "What the frick is that about?"

She texted back, "Relax, it's probably temporary".

"I replied, "One would hope!" then mused, "Perhaps the five cent drop in gasoline prices has finally hit me". I went on to say, "I almost feel like putting on a flouncy dress and running through the park singing "The Sound of Music."

She responded in turn, "Just as everyone suspected!", which actually made me laugh, another behavior I usually avoid before noon.

This was definitely becoming problematic.

Later that day, the expected nose dive never came. I was still feeling oddly "up", still riding this peculiar wave of optimism. I had finished my foray through the park proclaiming "the hills are indeed alive", which apparently is frowned upon by the local authorities...however I did get several nice complements on the flouncy dress.

After posting bail, I was still flush with goodwill, so I decided to drive up to a local garden center to pick up various flowers and tomato plants I promised Z I would attend to, facilitating our annual spring planting ritual.

See, I really was in a good mood! But then, on the way home, driving south on the highway, I happened to notice a HUGE billboard announcing: JUDGEMENT DAY IS COMING, MAY 21st, 2011!!!

And I say to myself, "What the %$#@*&! I finally start feeling happy and it's all going poof in 10 frickin days?!"

But then I think, maybe that's why I'm feeling so damn good.

No more pressure. No more impossible mountains to climb. No more Jersey Shore (the reality TV show, not the actual shore, which I happen to enjoy). It's all over; a week from Saturday!

So I rush home, do some research and this is the real deal. I mean, it's on-line and everything...and don't forget the billboard! Apparently the dead will rise and there's something about frogs, and evidently people with pink eye will be frowned upon.

Now, I'm feeling even more excited about life, or I guess I should say, after-life. I checked the whites of my eyes, which seemed to pass muster and figured I could get around that whole eternal damnation thing with a simple:

"Whaaaat...non-believer....me??? I was kidding! You knew that all along...right???"

And that makes me think, with all the excuse making that's bound to go on, what about all the processing and paper work that's got to be involved? I mean, imagine the lines. It really will be hell.

Anyway, my plan now is to max out all my credit cards and really live it up, I mean, while I can.

I've already fired off a whole slew of "in your face" e-mails to all the folks who've really ticked me off over the years, which as you can imagine is quite extensive.

I'm also cancelling my ENT appointment for Thursday; I'm just that serious.

So let the apocalyptic good times roll. And I've read it'll all be televised live, or whatever we'll be calling it, then.

It seems TV people have no chance of redemption and have to work.

May 22 - Uh oh...

Apparently it was all a mistake. Someone forgot to

carry a one. Multiplied when they were supposed to divide. Misplaced a decimal or dropped whatever it is clumsy theologians drop. Confused Isaac with Isaiah, which happens more than you'd think. It's not 2011...maybe its 2101!

Bottom line is: **I'M SCREWED!** But maybe not as much as the poor guy who spent his life savings putting up those damn billboards all over the country. I wonder if he budgeted taking them down. I'm guessing not. I mean, why would he?

In the end, "The End of Days" didn't mean the end of the world after all; it only meant the end of my good credit rating. How much do you think the minimum credit card payment is on $750,000.64? How many months will it take me to pay that off, even if I never spend another dime on anything?

And please...don't tell me until Kingdom Come. I guess I'll have to say goodbye to the llama, return the Ferrari and explain the odd smell coming from the back seat. Apologize to the French and replace my neighbor's prize gladiola bushes, which the lama seemed to find particularly enjoyable.

Anyone need a gently used Zeppelin?

Judgment Day, my...well, you know?

I guess anyone can make a mistake.

Live and let live...apparently.

Perspectives

I don't consider myself an artist but I do think I have

an artist's soul.

I mean literally...I think I have some if not all of van Gogh's soul. We were born on the same day 101 years apart, I'm very protective of my right ear and I have an acute aversion to crows and fields of crows.

Even the Counting Crows.

And I have to tell you, he left it in pretty piss poor condition, this soul. I've spent most of my life trying to patch all the holes in it.

To an artist, the world is all about perspective.

The unique way of interpreting what you see and how you see it, that nobody else in the world sees exactly the way you do.

Shadow and light, size and distance; even where, when and how you stand at any given moment...all affect perspective.

Everyone has their own perspective, though not everyone realizes it. Some realize it, but don't believe it's important enough to mention. Some realize it and believe it's important enough to mention, but have terrible memories and forget to mention it or forgot how to mention it, or where to begin.

But the artists, be they writers, painters, sculptors, musicians, dancers, photographers, nurses, teachers, doctors, masons, carpenters, laborers, accountants, lawyers (okay, definitely not the lawyers and I'm on the fence about the accountants) not only recognize their own perspective, but *NEED* to express it to the world in whatever unique way they can, in a way *ONLY* they can.

Except, like I said, the lawyers, who'll happily express themselves, anyway you'd like them to express themselves, then send you a bill.

And life—your life...my life...their life—is all about perspective, as well.

The places we were born.

The way we were nurtured, educated or not educated.

Whether or not we were forgotten and left behind in a rest room on I-90 when we were only 8 years old....

The friends we have, the friends we had, the friends we wish we didn't have.

The people we love. The people we don't. The people that don't love us (as foolish as that sounds).

Even our favorite ice cream or peculiar aversion to corn niblets, despite the fact we love corn on the cob...it all figures in.

Perspective...it's ours and only ours.

Most think we all live in the same world. I think we all live in different worlds. In fact, I think there are as many different worlds as there are people, and as many different universes as there are worlds...and so on and so on.

And I know many of you are thinking right now you're relieved you don't live in mine.

I think we sometimes get upset with our boss or our spouse or our kids or our friends because even though we're all looking at the same issue or thing, we're all looking at it from a different place, from a different time...from a different perspective.

Sometimes, what makes perfect sense to you is lost on me and vice versa...and versa vice.

But nobody knows exactly what's going on in your head (let alone mine) at any given moment, or what occurred in the past (and yes, I did say I was getting out at that rest stop and going to the bathroom!) that affects your perspective.

But we, too often, make the mistake of assuming everyone does or should know. And that's how we get into trouble. Nobody sees your perspective, not all the time; only you.

Yet, sometimes we do. Sometimes we click, and share part if not all of our perspective with someone else, and then we create Harmony, which is a beautiful thing, and should not be easily dismissed.

Unless, it's this woman, named Harmony, I once knew in college, whose parents were old hippies and well...let's just leave it at that.

It's just my perspective....

The Zombies Have Big Heads

Today is the dark of the moon, a day when it's said the veil between worlds is at its thinnest. Secrets from the other side are revealed to all willing to see...except the secret recipes for Coke, KFC & McDonald's special sauce.

It's also Halloween time and I have to tell you, the Zombies across the street have gotten big heads.

I mean what's left of their heads.

People are always taking shots at Zombie's heads because they're badly misunderstood. Ever since the *"Night of the Living Dead"* came out in 1968 people assume all Zombies are merely the undead walking aimlessly from town to town in search of human flesh.

I mean, there is some of that, but not to the extent people think.

They enjoy a nice vegetable dish with rice, from time to time, as well.

So people see Zombies walking down the street and what do they do? They remember the one silly line that stands out from all the rest.

"Kill the brain...kill the ghoul".

Anyway, they've gotten big heads because after a bit of a down period there's a resurgence of Zombies in films and TV; they're practically everywhere you look, these days.

So I guess they're entitled.

A couple of years ago it was the Vampires down the street who were doing all the howling.

"Finally," they said. *"People are seeing we're more than just peaked hairlines, bad teeth and capes with red satin linings!"*

And that's true...the Vampire woman down the street is just another soccer mom who waves hello every morning as she flies by the house after a night of bloodletting. And once you get past the fangs she has quite a nice smile.

I was talking to her husband one day—I think he works on Wall Street—while he was outside washing his coffin. He was telling me how hard it used to be for your average, run of the mill Vampire to get around without causing a flap. Now, he said, because of the recent popularity of all the Vampire books and movies, people at least recognize Vampires have feelings, just like everyone else. Say something disparaging to a Vampire and their hearts bleed, with or without a stake through it, just like yours and mine. Sure, the bloods a different color, but it hurts just the same.

And now they have to deal with all the Zombies shuffling around like they're the only ghouls in town.

To be honest, the Zombies across the street aren't as friendly as the Vampires by half. They really don't say a lot, and—I have to say it—they smell a little. I mean is there a rule or something that says a Zombie can't take a bath once in awhile?

There are five of them. A mom and a dad Zombie...I think, but with Zombies who can tell. Two teenage Zombies, a boy and a girl...again, I think. And I believe the mother-in-law/Grandma Zombie lives in the basement apartment. An illegal basement apartment, I should add, but who wants to get on the wrong side of the undead.

I don't even know any of the Zombies by name. My friend's daughter is in the same class with the girl Zombie, but she doesn't know her name either. She says all she does is sit there all day, looking bored, playing with her hair...after it falls out on the floor.

Once, while they were out, I snuck over to check their mail. I figured I could peek at a cable bill or something and catch a name, but that was a dead end. All I found was junk mail addressed: *To our Zombies at 1313 Mockingbird Lane.*

Junk mail...no one's immune.

So I continue to wave and say hello as they mow their lawn and walk their Zombie dog. Hey, just because they're rude doesn't mean I have to sink to their level.

I mean I kind of get where they're coming from. If people were constantly criticizing and taking shots at my head all the time, I would be a little standoffish too.

Besides, they're good to all the kids on Halloween who really get a kick out of them. They'll slump by the door, all night long, handing out all sorts of treats as long as the kids keep coming.

Sure, sometimes a wayward finger—and in rare instances a hand—snaps off and causes a bit of a stir, but hey, they're Zombies...get over it.

So I say, let the Zombies have their night in the moon. These things run in cycles; before we know it the werewolves will be back in vogue.

If it were you or me we'd be holding our heads high too.

Just not in our hands....

We Wuz Robbed!

Z has a habit of looking out the window into the front yard

whenever she gets up in the middle of the night to do whatever it is people do in the middle of the night.

She's been doing this going on 16 years now. For the most part, she takes a quick look and then goes back to bed.

Until the other night....

The other night she had the pleasure of spying a young man of about 18 –or as the police described him, *"male Caucasian, dark bushy hair, 18-20, navy blue T-shirt and green, possibly grey, baggy shorts heading in the direction of..."* well, you get the idea.

This wayward fellow was poking around in Z's car, looking for, I guess, her stash of Brooks & Dunn CD's.

I'm sound asleep since it's about 1 AM, so when Z wakes me to inform me of the situation my first instinct is to roll over and wish the fellow good luck sorting through the collected inventory of Z's car. Perhaps he might be able to find that pair of sneakers I lost in there in 05.

Then she tells me he's heading down the driveway toward my car and I immediately jump out of bed and call 911. No one is going to mess with my collection of Snapple tops!

Besides, if he gets into the backyard and into my garage, my leaf blower is in jeopardy.

A man must protect his leaf blower.

"911—what's your emergency?"

"Well I'm not really sure it qualifies as an emergency, officer, but my wife just spotted a kid in our driveway, poking around in her car".

"Do you have a description of the "perp"?"

Actually, I'm not sure if he said *"perp"* but I want to believe that he did, and it makes for a better story.

"No sir, it's kind of dark and I'm cowering in my bedroom window, so it's hard to see. But I'm concerned he's heading down the driveway and into my back yard towards the garage....where my leaf blower is."

"Gas or electric?"

"Uh...electric?"

"Hmmmm....I find gas gives you more power, not to mention mobility."

"Well, I find the electric 's not as noisy and has plenty of power for my needs."

In the meantime, Z 's standing there listening to this exchange thinking *her* situation is not being taken seriously enough.

She just doesn't understand there's a process involved.

"Okay, sir; suit yourself. I'll send a car over right away to check things out".

I tell Z, not to worry; it's under control and then proceed to pick out suitable crime scene attire, in case I end up dodging bullets or involved in some sort of high speed pursuit.

Plus, I'm stalling for time waiting for the cops to arrive before stepping foot outside.

Z peeks out the window again and finds the "*perp*", or someone we think is the "*perp*" who might be just some poor innocent kid walking home from his girlfriend's house, calmly crossing the street, pass under a street light and turn the corner of the street that runs "*perp*"-endicular into mine.

The police car pulls up and I wait a minute or two, just in case the fellow we saw is not the '*suspect*" and there is still the danger of an altercation with the real "*skel*" (This is so cool. I knew all those hours watching NYPD Blue would pay off someday!).

Z, still not understanding there's a process to these things yells out the window to the 12 year old police officer, who's standing around on the front lawn, scratching his head, that her husband is on the way down to fill him in...so now I have no choice but to get out there.

I rummage quickly through the hall closet but have no idea where my bullet proof vest is, so I have to go "*commando*"...so to speak.

I fill the young, but extremely polite and competent officer in on the situation and he tells me he took a quick look around and didn't see anything suspicious, except for the ineffective electric leaf blower in the garage.

In the meantime, he's barking information as to the suspect's "*twenty*" into his walkie talk (short for walkie talkie) and 2 more police cars zip by the house and tear around the corner in hot pursuit.

I take a walk over to check out Z's car and see the glove compartment open and report this fact to the officer, who peeks in the widow.

"*Wow...looks like he really ransacked the vehicle,*" the officer says.

I tell him, "*Uhm...no...this is pretty much what the inside of the car looks like on most days.*"

I grab the handle and open the door and immediately start berating myself for disturbing the crime scene.

Have I learned nothing from CSI?

"*Sorry,*" I tell the cop. "*I guess now they'll have to take my prints too to exclude them.*"

He smiles politely and informs me that the crime scene boys probably won't have to come out if we don't find anything of value missing, which there doesn't appear to be.

I inform him of my missing sneakers from 05 and he says he'll make a note for the report.

Z, after finally picking out her own police activity outfit, appears on the scene and inventories the car, since she's the only one who can decipher the puzzle of shopping bags, empty water bottles, umbrellas and assorted pairs of shoes, within.

She reports the only thing that appears missing is a small change purse she kept for parking meters and such. She thought there was about $4.65 in it.

And now I'm really irate....a confirmed victim of a heinous crime.

Eventually, we roll up the crime scene tape, which I insisted on, and everyone gets on with their lives.

Except for me...

Now I sleep with one eye open, which is very disturbing to Z as she finds it unsightly.

Somewhere, out in the night, there's a *"perp"* a *"skel"* a bushy haired wayward young man enjoying $4.65 that does not belong to him.

And to him I have one word of advice.

"If you can't do the time...don't do the crime...."

Reincarnation's

Not For Everybody

Reincarnation's not for everybody.

Mostly if you're still alive.

If you're still alive, reincarnation can wait awhile...or else it might get too confusing.

We've all seen and heard about people who say they've had a past life; having certain memories or talents that have passed over into their current lives.

There's always some young 3 year old prodigy who can play Mozart like, well...Mozart...or your cousin's 2 year old who strangely knew exactly where to find that wad of cash your great grandmother hid in that old sofa in the basement.

So I guess it must be true.

The thing is...how come most people, who talk about their past lives, always think they were someone famous, like Michelangelo, Joan of Arc, Cleopatra, George Washington, Amelia Earhart or even Maury Amsterdam.

No one was ever just some guy from Wisconsin who grew beets in Oshkosh for a living.

Could it be, *maybe,* you weren't really Pythagoras, after all. Maybe you were just the guy who did Pythagoras' laundry. The guy who actually worked up the famous theorem but never got credit for it because he mistakenly wrote it down on the back of Pythagoras' laundry bill it and gave it to him by mistake.

Why couldn't you be that guy?

Or the guy who told Lincoln *"Go on...go out and see a show tonight! It was a long war...you've earned a break".*

You could be him...right?

And of course no one ever considers that maybe—just maybe—they could have been some sort of a cockroach or something. I mean somebody had to be...right?

Do you think the cockroaches just come back, as what...flies?

Or maybe you'll be a cockroach in your next life.

Ahhhh...never thought of that, huh?

But you're thinking being a cockroach would be a major regression.

Not necessarily true; maybe it's a step up. For one, cost of living expense for cockroaches are almost non-existent. They don't own...and, for the most part, don't pay rent...and if they do it's negligible.

Cockroaches are not fussy eaters. They'll basically eat anything that's put in front of them, much like most of my in-laws...especially the guy-in-laws.

But everyone appreciates a good eater.

Crime in the cockroach community is among the lowest of all pests. You just don't see a cockroach taking a crumb that doesn't belong to him. It's part of their strong, moral, cockroach code.

And that's another thing...food. There's always plenty of free food left behind by over indulgent humans that a cockroach rarely has to order in, which is good cuz cockroaches are notoriously bad tippers.

Cockroaches aren't concerned about fashion. Just about any kind of exoskeleton suits them, and when they get tired of it they just molt and grow a new one.

And don't forget about that whole cockroach survival thing. It's said, after any sort of Armageddon like event, which folks seem to like to predict every few months or so, the cockroaches are the most likely species to survive.

Them and Newt Gingrich.

Not sure why.

I think it has something to do with the levels of radiation cockroaches are able to tolerate.

With Gingrich, I think it's more about a well-developed defense and denial mechanism.

In either case they'll both probably mutate over time and grow to enormous proportions with large heads and egos.

Maybe even run for president.

So cockroach...Gingrich.

Gingrich...cockroach.?

See, the cockroach scenario isn't looking half bad right now...is it?

The World That Astounds Me

I've mentioned a couple of times in passing, it was 10 years

ago that we moved into this house. So there are a lot of milestone reminders popping up these days, of all sorts.

In keeping with the theme of 10, it was also about 10 days ago, on the 2nd that I was standing on this deck that did not exist 10 years ago, BBQ-ing a steak for dinner.

BBQ is ways of life for us, all year long, but especially in the summer, so it was pretty much business as usual.

As I wandered away from the grill, surveying my domain, as is my wont, between sizzles, I happened to look down on the little redwood deck by the side of the garage that was here when we bought the place.

Now, I have looked down on that deck on countless occasions, on dozens of summer nights throughout the years, smile at all of Z's pretty flowers then usually return to tend the grill.

But this night was different. On this night, I was immediately flooded with a memory of standing down there, 10 years before, to the very same day, also BBQ-ing a steak, but for the very first time, in this house.

It had been only 3 days since we'd plunged head first into the murky waters of home ownership and believe me when I tell you, heads were still spinning and hearts were still pounding.

I should also tell you that conjuring that image of the much younger, much handsomer *(if that's at all possible)* me was not a particularly difficult task, because of a picture Z took that night to commemorate the occasion. However, while the photo's been stuck on the fridge for lo these many years, the thought on that night, that this was indeed the exact date, was not.

Whatever the reason, because of the picture or beyond the picture, I was suddenly struck with the notion that somewhere in the vast slipstream of time, I was still there, at that moment, still cooking that steak, wondering what was to come in the days and years ahead...besides my water pressure tank, which was sorely needed.

Needless to say, 9 days later there was a lot that came and a lot that changed...for all of us. But everyone knows that; experienced it and dealt with in their own way.

So this is not a discussion about any of that.

No, this is more of a metaphysical discussion, to which some will relate, and others will find trite and silly.

But hey, sometimes, at least to me, there's more safety to be found in things unknown, than in things familiar.

Anyway, as I stood there looking down onto the little deck where I had once positioned the old grill, I called on the memory of that time and envisioned the simplicity of the "*me*" back then.

There I stood, grilling that night, already trying to find a baseline in which I could find the new normal, at least in how it applied to us.

Z and I, after a lot of ups and downs, a lot of hoops to jump through and mountains to climb, had finally settled into a home of our own.

Remnants of past ownership still showed themselves in the form of smelly carpets and floors, mildew growing on the side of the garage, a cockeyed, clothesline whirly-gig that shouted the 70's if not the 60's and a variety of doggie toys and balls that lay scattered about in various nooks and crannies.

The lawn was a mixture of something green and something not so green, none of which would ever be mistaken for actual grass.

Yet, there I stood, cooking tong in hand, not much different than the way I stand now, wearing much the same clothes...even listening to the same old Met game on the same old radio I've had since the 80's.

More importantly, while I stood there that night, I recalled feeling for the very first time since the move, an absolute certainty, filled with contentment and peace that we had done the right thing. As if a benevolent spirit had flooded my being and filled it with a sense that everything was going to work out and be just fine.

Of course, as I said, a week and a couple of days later that notion was rocked, for all of us. Yet, throughout that period of such uncertainty on both a personal and global scale, that feeling of solid ground firmly beneath my feet never left. And maybe that's what the message was about.

I had been assured, and that was good enough for me.

So on this night, 10 years later, I stared deep into that now empty corner, saw the "*me*" of then, and conveyed those reassuring sentiments back into the past, from the "*me*" of now....

"*It's true...we made it...we're here and we're safe. And you will be too....*"

So...were those comforting feelings I received that night a gift from "*future me*," 10 years hence, to "*past me*"?

Are all those little voices we hear in our head from time to time, messages from our future "*selves*" looking back with amusement on our present "*selves*"?

Is even more "*future me*" the voice I hear, telling me right now..."*Whoa buddy, are you sure you want to be writing this crazy stuff for everyone to read...?*"

I don't know. But it's kind of cool to imagine that it is.

I like the idea of me watching out for me.

Of warning "*past me*" ...,

"*Stay away from the abdominizer...it's all a crock of—*"

Don't I owe myself that much?

Like I said...*I don't know.*

But, what I do know is, while I can't control the world that surrounds me...I can control the world that astounds me.

And that's good enough for me....

From 9/12/2011

AARP - Fix the Glitch!

AARP has a Glitch.

They've mistaken me for some kind of an "old" person and keep sending me information on how to go quietly into my goodnight...on water skis.

Granted, I'm not as young a "pup" as I used to be, but I still have a few stops to make before I get to 60; even though its close enough to bump my head on every time I sneeze...that is, unless I throw my back out.

We told ourselves, 40 was the new 30. 50 the new 40...and now, well, even the thought of 60...is just damn depressing.

Unless you're 65 or 70, let alone 80-90-100...I think you get the point.

People live a lot longer these days. Getting to 100 isn't the big thing it used to be. The Centurion softball league is having trouble finding fields for all its teams to play on this year. And forget about umpires. Who wants to argue with a 105 year old over balls and strikes, let alone tell him touching second base with his walker doesn't count...not until you get into the over 110 league.

My plan has always been to live until 120. Then I decided I wanted to be around for the tri-centennial, so I upped it to 125. I figured it would be cool to have Willard Scott interview me on the today show. Plus, I'm looking forward to the fireworks.

Sure, 60 is looming, but for the most part I feel great!

Just like I did in my 20s and 30s.

It's always been normal for me to jump out of bed in the morning and walk around the house like Groucho Marx for half an hour, give or take. And that excess patch of hair in my ears, I have to comb every day, is just a reserve to replace the ones missing from my head. And yeah, I do have to pee, again...what's your point?

To be honest, I even had a tough time turning 20.

"My growth plates are frozen!"

30- *"I can't be trusted anymore!"*

40- *"What do you mean my knee bends the wrong way?"*

50- *"AARP can get me a great deal on Depends!"*

At least we don't look as old as our parents and grandparents did at our age...right?

I mean, remember how grey and wrinkled they looked to us back then with our sharp 25 year old eyes.

We look in the mirror, now, and we look nothing like they did...even in their 40s.

But do you think that has something to do with the fact that our eyes are pretty much shot to shinola now and have a way of airbrushing our view?

We think we look like Rock Hudson and Elizabeth Taylor.

But to a teenager we look like Lurch and Grandmama.

And the hardest thing—the hardest lesson—about getting old, is seeing those before us, whom we once knew only as "young", turn "old".

"So that's where old people come from."

When you're a kid, the roles are clear.

There's you—young.

There's your parents—old.

There's your grandparents—really old.

And sometimes your great grandparents—really, really old.

Those were the actors in place when you walked on stage and their roles were ever so.

But as you get older those roles change.

Everyone gets pushed up by the eager generation behind. Suddenly the babies are 30 and the kids are 40, claiming that 40's the new 20.

But that's the beauty of where I am now. The beauty of 50 and beyond.

At 50 and beyond, I've covered enough distance that I can stand on a bit of a high hanging ledge, look back at where I was, and see how far I've come.

And the view ain't half bad.

I'm actually wiser and healthier...but definitely not wealthier.

Being wiser, I look back and see the changes that took place behind me, and the changes taking place in front of me. I appreciate that change is the only constant to be counted. And I'm sage enough to understand, while dreams are just dreams, they're the food that fuel our youth.

And I also see that where we *are* is where were *supposed* to be, and what we look like today, is what we were always *supposed* to look like.

The fact were actually here to do that...today and hopefully tomorrow, is every dream come true.

The young have energy and dreams. Hard bodies and a sense of invulnerability...not to mention a sense that their parents will continue to pay their cell phone and credit card bills on into perpetuity.

We have caffeine and contentment. Creping skin and life insurance. Name tags so we don't forget our friends names at parties. Mortgages, one two and three...and don't forget...AARP!

But most of all we have wisdom...to see the trail behind with a sizable measure of "youth" to tackle the trail ahead.

And that's a pretty cool thing.

And if my knee would stop barking....

And if AARP would fix the glitch in their mailing list....

But that *really* is a good deal on the Depends...and it never hurts to plan ahead....

Dental Delight

I went to the Dentist a couple of weeks ago.

I hadn't been for a while.

I'm not sure how long, but I spent about 10 minutes in the office next door before I realized I was in the wrong place.

I thought those stirrups were inappropriate for a simple checkup and a cleaning...so after about 15 minutes I put my pants back on and left.

Anyway, last time I was there, my dentist, who I'll call my dentist, was telling me about his softball team and skiing in Aspen.

Now he was telling me about his grandkids and new condo at the assisted living facility. Apparently there's a great spread at the happy hour.

So a lot had changed.

It takes a certain kind of person to be a dentist. To be honest I can't think of a more..."unsettling"...profession. I mean sticking your fingers in people's mouths all day, and then having them bite your fingers to boot.

I can't help it; I have a sensitive gag reflex.

If I was a dentist I'd be gagging all the time. So probably that's why I'm not. I doubt I'd have many returning customers. So it's just as well...because of the gagging.

Anyway, I'm happy to report...look ma, no cavities!

Which just annoys Z to no end.

Z is very meticulous about her teeth. She's got this special super-duper electric toothbrush that times the brushing. I think it even gives the time and temperature...and traffic and weather.

Then she does the whole flossing thing and actually sings to her teeth and tells them a story.

Nah, I'm kidding. She only sings. It takes her about 2 or 3 hours to get through the whole process.

I, on the other hand, pretty much just get up and check if any teeth fell out onto my pillow during the night. If not, I'm good to go.

So you can see why she'd get annoyed by my perfect assessment.

Actually, it wasn't so bad, going. Like I said, it gave me a chance to catch up on things. My Dentist asked if I had any problems, and once I finished telling him about the run in I had with the old lady at the grocery store, and the uncomfortable situation with the Zombies and the Witches, he asked if I had any problems with my teeth.

I said, not that I was aware of, since I have very little feeling up there.

So he told me to open wide and proceeded to pull my mouth open this way and that, until I felt like a carp stuck on a hook.

He asked if I wanted to watch what he was doing on TV since he had this cool little tooth cam device he was dying to use. I told him I'd rather watch Oprah than watch the inside of my mouth, but he misunderstood and showed me pictures of the inside of Oprah's mouth, which he had in a drawer for some reason. This of course made me gag. But Oprah usually has that effect on me.

So after a bit of poking and prodding, he took up a hammer and chisel and proceeded to clean my teeth. Of course he was nonchalant about the whole thing, except for the few times he shouted out, "Sweet mother of Satan's bastard child," which I found odd, and had the receptionist come in to certify authenticity or something.

There was some back and forth small talk about sports and such where he would ask me what I thought of the World Series this year.

And I would answer, *"grmplgh lutrefgu dou."*
Then he'd bring up politics and the conversation would get a little heated while he was making his points and the chisel would go flying.

Embarrassed, he'd apologize and start poking around again, and I would say, *"grmplgh lutrefgu dou."*

But could you blame me?

Eventually he took a few X-rays, well kind of. He uses these special kind of X-ray glasses he says let's him see through things. So he took a quick look and said I was good to go.

On the way out the receptionist asked if I wanted to set up my next appointment...and then we both had a good laugh.

What can I say? I'm in good tooth.

I think it might be all those caramel apples....

Connecting Pieces

A couple of stories back, I wrote about Reincarnation

and cockroaches.

Z said she didn't see that coming...the cockroaches, I mean.

I told her, I didn't either; you never see cockroaches coming...they just sort of happen.

She said *"Ahhhh...I thought so."*

Yeah...that's what happens sometimes with these things, at least to me, and not just with cockroaches. You start out, heading in one direction, and, before you know it, you get turned around and end up somewhere else before you even start on the path you had intended.

But that's okay...you always end up where you're supposed to be, anyway.

The thing is, I do have a sort of metaphysical bent. However the doctors say they can straighten that through surgery.

Oooops...*sorry*.

Did it again.

I guess I like to make fun of it because a lot of people think if you dabble in the unknown, there's a little bit unknown about you too. Like if you're really somebody they want petting their dog.

See...*again.*

I admit to having certain empathetic qualities, somewhat stronger than other folks. Like, I can always tell when something out of the ordinary is affecting someone in my small circle of friends. I suppose it can be attributed to just paying attention and observing, day to day. But I also seem to know when something's a little *"off"* with people I've never met before.

And I don't mean the chili dog they had for lunch that day.

I can also tell when they're being disingenuous or their outer persona belies what they're really thinking or feeling.

That sort of thing.

Which is not always such a good thing.

Especially if you want to *keep* your friends.

But it *can* be a good thing in the proper circumstances...actually a *very* good thing.

Like when you pass a stranger on the street, meet their eyes and just *know* this person holds some significance to you...maybe in some life, if not this one.

I'm not talking about romance or in a *"cupid's silly arrow"* kind of way; I just mean there's definitely some sort of connection there. It isn't related to gender or age or anything really. It could even be a baby in a stroller. There's just something there that joins together in that moment and sends some sort of subtle signal. So subtle that most of us just ignore it and keep on walking, most likely never to see that person again...at least in this life.

And then there are those people that you do experience this connection with and they *are* in your life—this life—in some form or another...to some extent or another.

It's these folks...the ones you feel so comfortable to be with, who always make you smile on the inside, even when you want to smack them on the outside, that I'm talking about. Whether it's just sharing a pitcher of beer in a bar, talking sports or dinner in a restaurant at a table of ten, talking colonoscopies, you know you're where you're supposed to be, with who you're supposed to be.

They can be the people you fall asleep with every night, or the people you only talk to on the phone or e-mail once in a while. You might see them all the time or you might only see them at a barbeque once or twice a year...or maybe never at all. If, for whatever reason, you don't see these people for a long period of time...even years...you don't think about the time lost when you do, you just connect the last second with the one at hand and never miss a beat.

Just like the stranger passing on the street...you know...there's something rare and precious there. Your molecules stick and your DNA dance. And if you're lucky enough to be in each other's lives, in whatever form that takes, you never want to let that go.

Connections...they're rare but they're there.

Are they from a past life or a future one?

I don't know and I don't really care.

I'm just happy to have them...even the ones I don't know about...yet.

The Zombies are Annoyed

So now the Zombies are annoyed with me.

Great...and just before Halloween.

Apparently they read my last story about their big heads and took offense.

Who knew they could even read?

Zombies...so sensitive.

You never hear a peep from the Vampires and nary a howl from the Werewolves. Maybe because I'm always complimenting the wolves' on their torn and tattered fashion sense.

Hey, it works for them. What can I say?

So the Mother-in-Law/Grandma Zombie shows up at my front door and rings the bell.

I thought it was the UPS guy, so imagine my surprise when I open the door and find Grandma Zombie standing there, decomposing all over my newspaper.

What now? I thought.

She didn't say anything; she just looked at me but I could tell there was some attitude.

And there's nothing worse than Zombie attitude...unless you're married....

So I stammered a bit and said, "I guess you read the piece, huh?

I think she may have nodded, but it's hard to tell since they move very cautiously in social situations.

"Look, it was just meant to be satirical. I don't really think that...sort of."

Z came out from the kitchen and shot me a look. She's always warning me about taking things too far. I could already hear what she was thinking, *what's wrong with you...I told you the Zombies were oversensitive!*

"Hello, there", Z says as she approached the door. "I was just making myself a cup of tea; come in and join me!"

I'm a bit stunned by all this cordiality from the woman who won't even answer the door to pay the pizza guy,

Now she's cozying up to Zombies?

"Sure," I follow up. "Come on in...I think we have some Halloween cookies too."

I felt a little stupid, but it was all I could think to say.

Grandma Zombie smiled...I think, and shuffled through the door and into the kitchen with Z.

I know it sounds terrible but all I kept thinking was...*I have a Zombie in my house...a Zombie!*

So we sat at the kitchen table, exchanging pleasantries as neighbor will do when they're getting to know one another. Z asked about her grandchildren and Grandma Zombie took out a few pictures she had in her purse.

You could see it'd been a very nice purse in its time, but now it was a little cracked and tattered.

Kind of like Grandma Zombie, but hey, who isn't?

Z made a fuss over the grandkid's pictures, but to be honest, I've seen better autopsy photos.

All the same, I expressed my approval as well.

"Cute kids. How old are they?"

How old are they? What a stupid question to ask the resurrected, I immediately thought, kicking myself.

Grandma Zombie just glanced at me with that look Zombies get sometimes. You know, the one that's a cross between confusion and disdain. Then she started licking her lips...so I passed her the cookies.

This went on for quite a while until the doorbell rang, again.

I was dying to—or trying not to—do anything to get out of there, so I jumped to my feet and said, perhaps a bit too enthusiastically, "I'll get it!"

Z just shook her head in that subtle way that no one can detect, except for me, so I hurried off to the door.

"Hi...we were conjuring up some holiday treats and thought we'd be good neighbors and bring you some!"

It was Hannah and Helga, the cute Witch couple from next door.

"Hey", I said, genuinely pleased to see them. "I haven't seen you Witches since the middle of summer. Where've you been keeping yourselves?"

Hannah handed me a colorful plate with an array of chocolate covered something on it; I couldn't tell if it was eye of newt or toe of frog. Last year they brought wool of bat and tongue of dog, and the year before that a delicious hell-broth boil and bubble that really hit the spot on a cool October day.

"Oh, you know how it is, with Witches these days. There was some last minute business that came up overseas, and with all the layoffs, there was no one else to handle it, so we had to fly off on a moment's notice."

I just nodded, but in truth I had no idea what kind of business the Witches were in and I wasn't in a hurry to find out. Sometimes it's better not knowing what the neighbors are up to...if you catch my drift.

"Hey, one of the Zombies from across the street is here having tea, why don't you come in and join us?'

Helga bristled at the word Zombie and said, "You let a Zombie into your house?"

Hannah added, "I thought I smelled something rotten."

I had no idea that there was such animosity between Witches and Zombies. I just thought they were all in the same boat and would naturally get along.

Not the case...uh uh.

Just then Z came around the corner with Grandma Zombie and you could suddenly cut the tension in the room with a silver knife.

There was this big ugly hiss, which, at first, I thought came from Z, since she's not as fond of the Witches as I am, but it actually came from Grandma Zombie, and I have to tell you it was a little pointed, if not just rude.

The Witches stiffened, made some odd hand gestures I wasn't familiar with and spoke a few phrases in a language also unfamiliar. Then they turned and walked off in a huff.

"Thanks for the treats!" I shouted after them, but they just kept walking and didn't acknowledge me.

Great, I thought. *Now the Witches are annoyed, too. What next, the Vampires?*

Once the sour aura had cleared the room, Z thanked Grandma Zombie for stopping by and said she hoped she could stop over someday and meet the Grandkids.

Grandma Zombie made some high pitched squealing noise that I took for agreement and we wished her a Happy Halloween as she shuffled up the walk.

She was nearly to her front door, across the street, when I noticed she had left one of her arms on the table, so I chased after her to return it.

Zombies...it's always something.

Our Smoking Ghost

We have a smoker in the house.

And since Z and I live here alone...and neither of us smokes....

Well, you can see where I'm going with this.

On any given Saturday evening, Z will be in the kitchen chopping away at some poor radish or cucumber or other unsuspecting salad making ingredient.

Believe me...you don't want to be a salad making ingredient in our kitchen.

I'll wander in, sniff the air and say, *"Someone's been smoking in here again"*. And Z will reply *"Yep"*...since Z is not a big talker while chopping, which is a good thing. Then she'll put down the knife, open the window and put on the exhaust fan.

This has been going on, intermittently, since our first Christmas, soon after we moved in, now almost 16 years ago.

At first we thought it was just some old smoking residue seeped into the walls, since time in memorial or hold over smoke from our pretty stone fireplace; but no...this was definitely tobacco smoke.

We poked around in all the corners, under and behind all the counters; even the basement ceiling tiles below. And none of that smelled like smoke.

So the only *"logical"* conclusion we could come to was...we had a ghost in the house...a smoking ghost to boot.

And while you might think, at first, as we did, this was undeniably a thoughtless, rude ghost, who refused to follow the norms and customs of *today,* by taking its filthy habit outside, you have to remember, ghosts operate under a different set of rules than us live folk. Plus, I'm guessing, smoking is probably quite common among the dead since, well, since they're already dead.

So the health risks are minimal.

Anyway, that's pretty much the extent of its ghostly activity. No tables moving, no chairs balancing on end or green slime oozing from the walls.

Just smoking.

So I guess it could be worse. I mean the ghost could be ordering pay per view, and it doesn't, so in that way it's a considerate ghost.

Interestingly, when we first moved into our humble little abode, we replaced the original oak floor in the dining room and found this old-fashioned tin for small cigars tucked under the old floor boards. So it must have been sitting there since at least 1927 when the house was built.

It got me wondering who put it there.

Obviously, one of the builders; but did he just misplace them or did he put them there thinking it would be cool for some folks in the future to find them?

But I don't think he would have said *"cool"*. He most likely would have said that would be the *"cat's pajamas"*, which is the kind of thing they said back then. I think it had something to do with the unfiltered water.

I tend to think it was the latter; since the box was empty..."*no cigar*" as it were. But it would have been the *"cat's pajamas"* if he had left a note from the *"past"* for us to find.

Even "*cat pajamier*" if it read, *"A fat guy named Lou left this on August 7ᵗʰ, 1927"*.

Or even better if it said, *"There's an annoying loudmouth named Lucille buried under your bathtub! August 7ᵗʰ, 1927"*.

Then I got to thinking about all the people who lived in this house; the house I now own, but really just reside.

In truth, we're only the 3ʳᵈ set of owners. The previous ones lived here from 1972-2001. Besides the funky Laugh-In style wallpaper they left under the funky treasure chest stove hood thing in the kitchen, plus a lot of graffiti in the boiler room, they didn't leave behind anything of much significance...at least to me.

It's the original owners, who lived here from 1927-1972, more than half the life of this house, who come to mind when I think about the past, and feel their presence.

Think about all they lived through, right here.

All the happiness and all the sadness that comes with a life, right here.

A Model T parked in the driveway. The ice man cometh. The milkman goeth. The Depression, Prohibition, Al Capone, Dillinger, Bonnie and Clyde, those funny crank style telephones, party lines, a farm down the street, trolley tracks, radio soap operas, Little Orphan Annie, two World's Fairs, one World War, rationing, blackout curtains. Coolidge, Hoover, FDR, Give em Hell Harry, Eisenhower, JFK, LBJ, NIXON!!! Those poofee women hairdos, those slicked back men's hairdos, crew cuts, shag cuts, Korea, Vietnam, Sinatra, Goodman, Miller, Elvis, The Beatles, B&W TV, Color TV, rotary phones, Princess phones...and of course my recently departed beautiful porcelain relic of a slop sink.

These are the things I think about as I tend to my fire on a cold winter night and imagine it's 1927 and we're all sitting close to the coals, trying to stay warm.

Me, Z and our smoking ghost.

They Made Me Be The Judge!

A while back I was summoned to County Court to serve

my sentence...I mean jury duty.

A very large group of us were brought up to a very large judicial room, with a very large judicial bench, at which a very large judicial judge eventually sat down. We were shown a short video hosted by some actor whose name eludes me, but probably wasn't Robert Blake, the former Little Rascal, and star of the mid 1970's TV show Baretta, who was tried and acquitted of killing his wife in 2001.

But maybe it was....

After the movie, we were then entertained by a raffle in which the prizes were apparently us. If your juror number was pulled from the rolling cage, you had to stand up, and if you didn't trip on the way down to the front of the room, you were awarded to the attorneys looking to seat a jury, and hauled away.

I figured this was an excellent development since I've never won any sort of raffle in my life. So what were the odds?

Right...on the very last number called...I finally win! An all expense trip to the jury room to be questioned as to my juror capabilities.

And then I win again, since after many questions and back and forth, I am also the last juror selected for this particular case.

Despite our whining, we are all congratulated for our civic pride and told to go home for the weekend, speak of our experiences to no one, and return on Tuesday, bright eyed and bunny tailed, since this was also Easter weekend and the bailiff was desperately trying to infuse us with holiday spirit. I believe a secret handshake may have been involved, as well.

So, on the appointed Tuesday we find ourselves, civically proud, back in County Court, sitting in a small, musty juror's room, waiting to be called in to render justice in the matter of an elderly woman who was being sued for hitting a younger woman with her car...or vice versa. The facts elude me at this time, as well as they did then, but I was not about to let that stand in the way of justice. I mean woman, old or young, versus car, made in the USA or import, it's no contest, right? I mean what's the defense..."She had it coming, your honor?"

The facts, muddled or not, were clear...at least to me. Even though I did know a few people that I would gladly...but I digress.

Sitting there, observing my fellow jurors while away the time, my mind begins to wander, as my mind is prone to do. I am somewhat jealous of my mind in that regard, since as usual, I am forced to stay behind.

The next thing I know I'm sitting in the courtroom. The trial has finally begun.

Hours passed, yet time seemed suspended. It was only later we were told the official court room clock had been broken since 1962.

The arguments were coming at a fast and furious pace. Our heads, bounced back and forth like ping pong balls. But then, suddenly, without warning, which would tend to indicate suddenness, in and of itself, the judge gasps, grabs his chest, and plummets from the bench.

THUNK!

Everyone rushed to his side, because the very sound of the Italicized, Bold, Capitalized **THUNK!** told us this was indeed serious. However, we were quickly assured by the bailiff that this was a common occurrence, especially on this bench, especially after post-holiday dinners featuring Fettuccine Alfredo.

A sigh a relief rushed across the crowded court room, but apparently the judge was finished for the day.

A cloud of confusion now descended as we all stood around wondering how we could go on. The Lawyers continued to argue, possibly about lunch, while the old lady grabbed the young girl, and tossed her to the courtroom floor, screaming, "I'll show you who's got a bad back, now, you little—!"

Anarchy ruled the day. Something had to be done.

Luckily, my fellow jurors and I had bonded into a close knit group, having earlier defeated several of the other Juries, in the Juror's lounge, in hotly contested leg wrestling matches.

We had faced all comers and proved victorious in all.

Naturally, my fellow jurors turned to me, in this hour of their most dire need, as I had proven myself to be the strongest and bravest of all leg combatants. It seemed reasonable to assume I was naturally the wisest and, without saying, which I'm sure was an oversight, the best looking of the lot.

"Please, wise and moderately handsome one," they beseeched. "You must lead us to a wise and moderately fair decision so that we may ultimately be set free."

Alas, I relented, how could I not, but with one non-negotiable proviso. In order to add spice to the case I required that the attorneys must now present the remainder of their arguments in song and dance.

My fellow jurors gasped in appreciation, as the testimony had grown tedious and dry.

So off to the judge's chambers I was escorted, where I was given my official judicial robe to don. I was not too pleased with the fit, which fell several inches above my knees, and the back constantly flew open as I walked, which normally would not have been a problem, had I been told I was allowed to keep the remainder of my street clothes on.

Who knew?

I took to the regal judicial bench, sticking to the regal judicial synthetic, Naugahyde chair...and the proceedings began.

I listened patiently for several seconds until at last, I gaveled the arguments to a halt, saying I'd grown weary of these same old song and dance routines, and besides, the synthetic Naugahyde chair was giving me a very nasty rash.

I directed the bailiff to procure an ointment and ordered the plaintiff and defendant to continue their wrestling match to determine the outcome.

Two out of three falls was decreed.

In the meantime I ordered the two attorneys to be sentenced to 10 years of jury duty and the wearing of judicial robes for several days, without pants.

Court Dismissed....

But in the real world, when my mind finally returned from wandering, we waited quietly from 10:15 to 11:30 in the jury room outside the court. There, we sat, "Twelve Angry Men" (and women, except there were only eight of us) and we're told this was our home until the case was decided.

Great, we thought.

Then the real judge walked in wearing a sheepish expression. He explained, the plaintiff was ill and the trial wouldn't start until Thursday.

Many looks of disdain flew around the room.

The judge then said he wouldn't expect any of us to be on call for that amount of time, and declaring himself a "Juror's Judge", said we could all be excused if we so desired and be exempt for the next four years.

We all looked at each other wondering what the catch was, and then, as a unit, bolted for the door.

The Marshall, assigned to guard us asked, "Are you sure you all want to go?"

We were....

Saved by the Bell

I get all kinds of doorbell visitors.

Phone companies, magazine and candy salesman. High School Band members, cheerleaders. gas and electric suppliers, politicians and young kids who are intent on saving the environment, but not so much concerned about polluting the neighborhood.

And in most every instance I cut them off very quickly, tell them I'm not interested and turn them away.

And to be honest I kind of enjoy watching those smiles turn upside down.

But sometimes I do offer them a bottle of water on a very hot day...especially the environmentalist, because they tend to get crankier than the others.

About once every month or so, a couple of Church Ladies ring my doorbell to say hello, hand me a couple of their latest publications, and attempt to save my misbegotten soul.

Oh, and they come to laugh, because saving souls can be a bit of a downer most of the time.

When they come to save me, though, they know it will at least be a good time for all.

They're nice people. And they put up with me, who can be...well, let's say difficult...when it comes to people talking to me about religion.

One of the nice ladies is always the same, but she seems to bring a new partner every time.

I guess I'm an acquired taste, even in soul saving endeavors.

I've given my views when it comes to all things theological, here before, so I'll spare you any discourse now. But the Church Lady first arrived at my door not long after we moved here.

I had seen her in the neighborhood walking from door to door on a hot sticky Saturday afternoon, that first summer, and she was receiving a less than welcome reception from most of the places she'd been.

Whereas I would probably have been ripping flowers from people gardens on the way out, this effervescent woman was always smiling, undeterred from her mission.

When she showed up at my door, I did what was only natural....I threw myself on the floor and crawled behind the couch.

The only problem was the front door was open, and since I had also knocked over a lamp, she was *yoo hooing* through the screen, asking if everything was alright in there....

So I mustered a big smile, crawled out from behind the couch and went to meet my maker, or at least a very good friend of my maker.

I politely listened to her spiel, which to be honest was very short and to the point. I told her how much I admired what she was doing; her dedication and above all her patience with some of my less than hospitable new neighbors. I told her if I was running heaven, which I hoped to someday, I would make sure she got a room with a view and possibly even a swimming pool, while my neighbors would be relegated to split levels in the Heavenly equivalent of Levittown, NY.

That earned me a great big belly laugh, mostly because I don't think she was expecting it, and I actually caught some of the neighbors peeking through their curtains wondering just what kind of person had taken up residence on their block.

I then proceeded to make very clear that while I certainly had my views on spirituality and religions of all kinds—some positive, most negative—I had talked it all to death, was very happy where I was in that regard, but I'd be happy to have her drop by and leave her reading material, if that was of any benefit to her. But no discussions, no bible thumping and especially no praying for my obstinate soul.

This pleased her to no end, and she told me that was a much better deal than she gets at most places, so she would see me in a month.

And she did, and she did...and she still does, when I'm not hiding behind the couch, almost every month, for about 10 years; but, like I said, with a different partner each time.

I think it's how they break in the new people. Or punish the old people.

Not sure....

The first time she returned, she called me by name so I asked her if Jesus had told her my name...or if she had written it down.

She immediately burst out in that great big window rattling laugh of hers and admitted she had written it down.

Again the neighbors were peeking out the windows.

Again she handed me her little magazines.

Most times I get a little spiel on the hot topic of the month, to which I nod my head a lot, then comment on what a good looking savior they have pictured on the cover. I tell her I didn't know Jesus looked so much like James Brolin, or that he was able to afford 200 dollar haircuts.

This elicits another big laugh from my friend, and a horrified expression from her partner who usually starts to wave various herbs and preventative talismans in my direction.

And then she's gone until the next soul lifting moment....for both her and for me.

Most of my friends are befuddled when they learn about this and just how long it's been going on.

They think I'm the last person they know who would allow such an invasion of time and space.

But I tell them, I don't mind at all, and since all that's asked of me is that I listen to what she has to say for 30 seconds and take a glance at her magazines to see if anything strikes my fancy. How can I not have time for that?

My friend, the Church Lady, is the one putting in all the time. It doesn't matter if I think it's time well spent or not.

So she wants to save my soul....what's wrong with that?

To be honest it could use a good scrubbing.

So the next time you're doorbell rings, don't be so quick to go visit the dust bunnies behind the couch.

And there's no law here or above—or even below—that says you can't laugh about it.

Is there...?

Stared Senseless

I often catch people staring at me.

I'd like to think it's because of my matinee idol looks, but I think it's more because of my one uneven nostril.

I never thought it was that noticeable, but I guess it is.

And it's not like I'm laying traps trying to catch people staring at me...I'm not...but a lot of times I'll look up from what I'm doing and there they are...staring.

Maybe staring is the wrong word. It's not like they're there with their mouths agape, or fallen to their knees muttering.

I suppose it's more of a quick glance.

And then they turn their heads away, real quick, as if someone across the room just slipped on a banana peel.

But by then it's too late; I've already spotted them.

Once you make eye contact, you've been made.

And it works the opposite way as well.

If you're staring at someone and they look up at you, make eye contact, even if just for a millisecond, looking away only makes you look guilty of something...like maybe dropping the banana peel.

But we all do it...and none of us ever call the starer on it; probably because in some way we're all a little flattered...until we look in the mirror later and discover that small piece of rigatoni stuck to our cheek.

Late night snack mishap; I thought I'd gotten most of it off my pillow....

And why is it that if you do happen to come upon someone who catches your eye, for whatever reason, even if they're 20 feet away, the second your focus lingers on them a moment too long, they look up?

And we do it too, if someone is staring at us...you know, because of the dried pasta.

What's that about?

And they say we only have five basic senses.

I say we a have a lot more than that.

Like the sense that someone ate the last fig newton...I get that one all the time.

Or the sense you probably should buy new socks and underwear, especially after a couple of decades have past.

But that's certainly a relative thing...and I'm not talking about any specific relative...honest, I'm not.

There's also the sense you get that someone is talking about you...especially when you walk into a room and the conversation cuts off in mid-sentence, and everyone looks at you and shakes their head.

But that's more of an acquired sense...not everyone develops that one right away.

How about the sense that the traffic light you see up ahead that's been green forever is going to turn yellow just as soon as you get about 8 feet from it and the car ahead of you goes through it.

Or the impending rain shower that's been threatening all day will hold off just long enough for you to roll your grocery cart out of the supermarket and out to your car, which is located about a half mile away.

Or the sense you have you mixed up the date of your friend's birthday party after you show up at the appointed time, and your friend answers the door in a skimpy negligee and curlers, even though he said he was past that, and tells you you're a month late...but thanks for the card...two years ago.

Or the sense you're probably getting right now that most of this is really just non-sense, and you would've been better off if you had checked out the Weather Channel instead.

Yeah that's a pretty good sense too....

What are you staring at?

Springtime Renewal

It's springtime in our little corner of the world and to a lot of different people that means a lot of different things.

For those who observe Easter and Passover it's a time of solemn religious significance, and for others it's a time for bonnets, bunnies and colorful eggs.

No matter what your belief system or non-belief system, the common thread that runs through all of it is renewal. And I don't mean renewing your beach permit, car registration, health club membership or your subscription to Sports Illustrated and or Martha Stewart Living.

I'm referring to the renewal of life in whatever form or symbolism you subscribe to.

If you're a person who doesn't subscribe to any organized religion, or even any of the disorganized ones, you'll find renewal all around you through the scent of awakening earth, the promise of budding trees and fulfillment of blooming daffodils.

I include myself in this latter category of spring revelers. I'm in no way religious, but in the chi chi modern, new age vernacular I guess you would say I am somewhat spiritual in my beliefs.

Yeah...I know.

I recently heard someone say on a TV show I was watching that religion is for those who seek salvation and spirituality is for those who seek answers. It might have been on *"Lizard Lick Towing"* or *"Hoarding: Buried Alive"*...not sure which...but it was on TV so it must be true.

Truth is, I'm not really looking for answers—at least any more—and Z says I'm beyond saving in any way, shape or form.

It's not that I'm without any sense of universal truth inside; I do believe there is some sort of order to things and those things do make sense on some mysterious level.

I also believe there's something greater than me responsible for that order and sense.

For a while I thought it was Trump...then he came out with the *"Celebrity Apprentice"* and that was the end of that.

Then I thought it must be Oprah, but her new cable network isn't doing all that well, so now I'm kind of at a cross roads.

I don't know...and I guess that's the key: *I don't know*...and never will...at least in *this* life.

But at the risk of sounding much too Zenny, I do know I don't *need* to know either.

It's enough for me to feel that there is "something" and some form of "existence", be it unknown, that makes sense and lives on through all of us long after this life concludes.

Hopefully, with much better 3D-TV technology.

Bottom line is...breathe in the spring that surrounds us this time of year and enjoy your holiday, whichever that may be.

No matter what you believe or don't believe, this time of year is a time of celebration... of life and life renewed for all of us.

Enjoy all the food and all the togetherness your tradition brings to your table.

Enjoy your family and your friends and all the love and laughter they bring to your life.

Most of all, take pride in and enjoy that which you believe and *feel* in your heart to be true, with respect and acceptance of all that you don't.

Even the Easter Bunny...because I've been trying to figure that one out since I was five....

There's Always Some Nun to Blame

I've mentioned a time or two, I attended Catholic Grammar

school, full time, from 1960-1968, so I spent much of my early life surrounded by nuns.

Hey, why wouldn't I?

Nuns are great....

We'd hang out at the convent to all hours, listening to the latest from Dylan; debating if this whole British Invasion thing was going to take off or wondering why no one really knew which of the five was actually Dave Clark.

Good times!

Well...not really....

I mean maybe if we actually did those kinds of things, but we didn't.

Mostly we showed up every morning, sat quietly, hands precisely folded at the edge of our desks, backs straight, feet flat on the floor, and tried not to make eye contact with them.

Making eye contact was bad.

Making eye contact meant you were *noticed* and might be called on.

Being called on was bad.

Being called on meant you had to respond to the question being posed, and if your mind had chosen just that moment to wander back to the perplexing theories being proffered by Captain Kangaroo, earlier that morning, on hot cereal vs. cold...you had a problem.

See, the nuns of that era, had a theory of their own, which was that a little bit of pain was a good thing to get the old brain power in gear. Not enough to draw blood or leave a mark, but just enough to help you recall those pesky times tables.

We had a nun, in the first grade, named Sister Helen, which may or may not have been her real name.

I suspected at the time her real name might actually have been Natasha, and that she was a secret agent for the KGB who pal'd around with Boris Badenov.

That's what I suspected.

Anyway, if you weren't able to respond in the proper hands precisely folded at the edge of your desk, back straight, feet flat on the floor manner that was expected, "*Sister Helen*", who was fairly youngish by nunish standards, would sidle up behind you—because they were experts at sidling—and grab hold of the one, precise little hair on the back of your head that was connected to every single nerve in your body...and pull.

Never could you imagine that one little hair could be the source of such pain.

Now, panicked and totally clueless as to the nature of the question posed, you begin to throw out anything that pops into your head. Numbers, letters, historical figures and dates, bodies of water, continents...major and minor exports *and* imports of Brazil. Anything and everything, hoping against hope by some miracle you'll hit on the correct answer.

But you never did and the pain would continue until eventually a bright light would appear, beckoning to you, calling you home, bringing you some measure of peace, until you realized it was just Mrs. Gordon, the cleaning lady, opening the door to the cloak room, where we stored all our cloaks when we weren't using them.

The dagger room was in the back.

Then, to further add to your humiliation, Sister "*Natasha*" would keep on tugging until someone *was* finally able to answer the question, which was usually *Marybuttercup Pennyloafers*, with her smug little smile, who always had the answer to everything...including what exactly happened to Marilyn Monroe.

And then the pain would stop; at least the physical pain.

To be honest, I guess it could have been worse. This was pretty much as deep as Sister Helen's bag of tricks went. For the most part she was nice to us as long as we were paying attention.

She had birthday parties for us with cupcakes, and holiday games and celebrations, exercise time when we would open all the windows on a 4 degree day, breathe in and breathe out, stretch and touch our toes.

She would even let us smoke in the back of the room....

No...I'm kidding.

We had to go outside to smoke.

So Sister Helen wasn't so bad.

Some of the other nuns, and to be fair, lay teachers, I had along the way—those primarily left over from the Mesolithic era, when corporal punishment was widely accepted and expected—incorporated teaching methods that would have been frowned upon, even by Boris and the KGB.

But that was the way of the world before us, and even if our parents had a problem with it, there was a definite *"ask me no questions and I'll tell you no lies"* policy in place.

In stark contrast to today, where if a teacher even hurts a kid's feelings, they could be brought up on charges.

Someday down the road I'll tell you about my 100 year old, or so it seemed, 4th grade teacher, a bull of a woman, who blamed us for the untimely death, over the summer, of our 150 year old 3rd grade teacher. She told us we may have *gotten* Mrs. Cooney, but we weren't going to *get* her....

Oh, and she also blamed us for killing President Kennedy.

Yep...marched right in after they announced it on the PA system, which was out and up the hall, so it was mostly unintelligible to us, and said, *"The President is dead and it's all your fault because you were talking instead of listening!"*

And then we all felt bad about it.

I still do....

But don't tell anybody.

Especially Oliver Stone....

Directionally Speaking

I'm a little stubborn when it comes to asking for directions.

In the past, I would happily drive in circles, or drive 40 miles in the wrong direction, before I'd finally give in, turn the car around and get myself back to where I started...only to drive 40 miles in the other direction.

But maybe that's just a guy thing.

Or maybe just *this* guy's thing.

Not sure.

What I am sure about is, I don't like to ask for directions...and Z tends to frown on that...a lot...among the various other things she does to express her displeasure with this behavior...like jumping out of the car and calling for a cab.

But, ever since I downloaded my GPS, Michele, to my phone, those types of problems are pretty much behind us.

Plus Michelle is a cheap date on road trips.

She always orders from the Prix Fixe menu.

On the other hand, it might surprise you to learn if someone stops and asks *me* for directions, I'm very cordial and considerate—to a fault—towards any and all wayward travelers that happen to cross my path.

And I get stopped *A LOT*...mostly because I'm out on the road walking once or twice a day...and for some reason people think walkers are the towns Sherpas.

So I take my responsibility *very* seriously...mapping out in my head, not just the quickest route, but the easiest route as well.

If I've learned anything from Michelle, I've learned the best route is not always the easiest...especially if it involves driving under water.

I take my responsibility so seriously, in fact, at first there's always a short brain freeze period, when I'm not even sure what street I'm standing on.

Then...panicked, I start to spew out the names of any street and locale I can think of, trying desperately to get my bearings.

However, sometimes these streets and locales might not even be located in this country, let alone this town, so it can instill a little doubt in the misdirected driver's eye.

"Are you sure I turn east at the Berlin Wall?"

Usually, after a few uncomfortable seconds, I'm able to right myself. Plus, I find if I offer them coffee and a nice selection of pastry—which I always carry in a fanny pack, just for this reason—I'm able to regain their confidence, pretty quickly.

Of course, once I pass along my directional wisdom and send them on their way, I immediately start to doubt myself and begin to worry that maybe I wasn't as clear as I could've been.

Did I tell them two lights or three?

Will they count the light at the corner as one, or ignore it and start at the next light?

If they turn at the second light instead of the third, will they know enough to bear right at the stop sign?

Or will they think the third light is really the second light and stop at the bear?

Did I tell them to make a U turn before they start?

If they do get lost, will they think poorly of me and mock me to the bear...again?

So you can see why I don't like to ask for directions.

Besides...who am I to put that kind of pressure on a person....

Now if I can only remember where I left Michelle.

Hate the Breeze

There's a pretty stiff breeze blowing today.

Hate the breeze

The problem with the *"breeze"* is...at times it's more of a gale.

I like to take a long walk, once or twice a day, you know, *as part of the "creative process",* and given the ferocity of this *"breeze"* one really needs to be on the alert.

There's a distinct danger of being blindsided by small flying objects such as tree branches, hats, umbrellas, newspapers, rigatoni, potted plants and the occasional small dog.

It's very disturbing to be strolling along, lost in one's thoughts, only to be bonked on the head by a Beagle...especially if the Beagle has a mouth full of rigatoni.

And it makes it difficult to proffer the compulsory phony greeting to one's fellow walkers if one is constantly dodging last week's recycling.

If you're a walker, you know exactly what I mean by the phony greeting. The thing that acknowledges the natural, yet unspoken, camaraderie amongst walkers. The thing that says, *"Hey, you don't want to die prematurely either!"*

But this camaraderie extends only so far as the trail unfolds. Put us on line together at the grocery store and we won't even look each other in the eye; unless it's to give one or the other "malocchio", the evil eye, for bringing 13 items to the 12 item lane. However, like I said, put us on a wooded path, or sunny lane and we're smiling and waving to each other like happy fools who hadn't seen another soul in over a year.

Of course, like most things, this walker's acknowledgement, like walkers themselves, can take many forms.

There's the serious walker, focused, goal oriented, arms pumping, along with synchronistic strides, who will only acknowledge you with a subtle nod of the head.

There's the happy wanderer, quietly humming, scanning the trees and surveying the skies, who greets you with a verbal hug, a weather report and the current bunny count, out on the trail. They'll also correct your greeting from "good morning" to "good afternoon" because they're not fond of inaccuracy in any form.

There's the barking dog walker (The dog barks, not the walker) who not only acknowledges you with a great big sheepish smile, but also the fact that their yapping, growling, snapping dog is just a great big coward at heart...and most likely doesn't have rabies, even if that is more than just a flesh wound.

And speaking of yapping, I would be remiss if I didn't acknowledge the people "yappers" who walk in pairs and yap yap

yap about their kids, their jobs, their wives, their husbands and anything else that one is prone to yap about.

You sometimes feel as if it would be rude to interrupt the yappers, but as if on cue, at the precise appropriate distance (which is also a source of debate. 10 ft. too far...3ft. too close?) they'll suddenly stop yapping in mid-sentence, smile and proffer a simple, yet polite, "hello", then immediately pick up the yap right where they left off.

And I won't even discuss those poor, solitary, miserable individuals who in their poor, solitary, miserable way, refuse to make eye contact and walk right by as if you were trying to sell them insurance. But don't be fooled...we know who you are, and you are on the list....

And what about the " *Return Loopers*"? You know, like when you're walking a circuitous loop and you pass somebody going in the opposite direction. You extend your salutation of choice, comment on the day and pretty much use up all your good greeting material. Then about twenty minutes later...here they come again.

So now, an awkward moment ensues. There's enough of a distance between you, as you approach, that the uncertainty morphs into panic. Desperately, you try to recall just what form of acknowledgement you previously extended. If it was the big hello, are you safe with just the subtle nod? Is a weather reference in order, or did you use that already? Do you make a joke about having to stop meeting like this, and risk appearing imbecilic? Do you wave from a distance, acknowledging the kismet inherent in the situation, or casually avert your eyes until the very last second then grunt something unintelligible and quickly move away?

So you see, there's a lot to contend with on a simple afternoon stroll; so much more I can barely touch upon here.

There are the passing car honkers who zoom by at 50 miles an hour, expecting you to recognize their protruding elbows as they wave.

There are the iPod joggers, who sneak up from behind and startle you into the bushes.

The sidewalk bikers who beseech you with expressions of sheer terror to jump off into the street, because you'll have a better chance against a 10 ton, moving truck than you will against them. Not to mention pot holes, cracked sidewalks, bird poop, dog poop, coyotes and did I mention coyote poop.

So you can see why, with all of that...I really hate the breeze....

The House That Still Haunts

There's something weird about me.

Okay...I see the heads nodding out there.

I also see your point....but that's not what I mean.

What I mean is, I seem to absorb whatever sense of history exists in a place wherever and whenever I come across it.

The obvious are places of historical significance like Ellis Island, the remnants of Thoreau's little house in the Woods or famous battlefields, like my grandparent's old house.

I think everyone gets some sort of vibe from those places; they've come prepared for that so they're already open to it.

No...I'm talking more about your average, everyday encounter with the past in everyday situations.

For instance, whenever I walk down Main Street in my little hometown, I pick up all sorts of things; not including the parking ticket left on my windshield during the 30 seconds it took me to walk down to the new and improved fancy shmancy central parking pay station thingie.

No...not including that.

Most of the buildings downtown date back to the early to mid-19th century. Even before that, these same streets bustled with all sorts of commerce schlepping back and forth to the schooners tied up in port.

So when I'm strolling through the village, I pretty much shut out all the hub bub taking place in all the fine international dining establishments, check cashing services, long distance phone stores and other small retail businesses that have taken up residence in those old spaces and just soak up the ripples from the past.

I see shop owners squeegeeing store front windows clean and sweeping street dust off the sidewalks. There are horse drawn carts carrying logs to the saw pit and carriages carrying people to the shops. An old fire pumper rolls down the street as men, dapper in bowlers and cravats, ladies, sublime in bodices and skirts, stroll the streets after lunch. The butcher, still in his blood stained apron converses with the shoe maker, his fingers hopelessly blackened with shoe polish.

I don't know where this comes from, really. Just echoes from the past, I guess.

When I was a kid, there was no one place that resonated with these echoes more than an old deserted mansion, set back on an isolated hilltop, up in the woods on the edge of town. There were actually two of these huge houses, one a bit smaller than the other, both of which we called haunted, because to a 10 year old that's exactly what we wanted them to be. I imagine, at one time, they served somebody well, but right at that particular time they served to pretty much scare the *bejujus* out of us.

One by one, we'd sneak through the woods and approach the house from behind this low stone wall that I guess served as a long ago boundary marker. From there, we'd peek to see if there was anyone in sight.

If the coast was clear, one of us would give the signal and up over the wall we would fly, making a mad dash for the front porch and door.

Then suddenly...*we were in!*

I'm talking in your classic *"Vincent Price"* haunted mansion here, except the only ghosts around were in our heads. But believe me...*that was more than enough.*

Today, it boggles my mind to even think that this place actually existed. Even more, that we actually had the cajones to go inside, which now that I think of it, was probably trespassing and a violation of several laws. So, for the remainder of this story, let's just say this is all *hypothetical.*

Okay?

So *"hypothetically"* speaking, I recall the main hall housing the remnants of an old baby grand piano, just sitting there, keys missing, along with one leg, or maybe it was two. In fact, it might have been merely a small upright piano, but baby grand is more impressive, so that's what I recall.

Wall sconces, equally spaced, graced the large room, which was divided into sections by tall, foggy windows, some of their panes long gone, other cracked and broken. There was even what we called a *secret doorway*, a discreet opening that blended into the wall, which lead to what we thought of as a secret passage and stairway that snaked through the interior of the house.

Of course there was also the ruin of an old chandelier, at least, again, in my memory, that lay in the center of the room and a staircase so majestic that one expected Scarlet O'Hara to come sweeping down from above.

Once inside the house, we proceeded to spook each other with every ethereal squeak and groan of the floorboards and the real or imagined sounds of car doors slamming...*they were coming to get us!*

In and out of rooms we'd go, some stripped bare, except for a coating of time, others decorated with empty beer cans and bottles, undoubtedly the product of another sort of activity that took place by night with kids somewhat older than we.

Some rooms even showed signs of transient habitation; a refuge on a cold winter night for some unfortunate, I suppose.

Were they lurking somewhere behind the walls, peering out at us, pick ax at the ready?

No...but we liked to think that maybe they were.

Sometimes we'd venture into the attic, a somewhat cramped space for such a big house, and there we'd discover old hangers from a local cleaner—back when phone numbers featured far less numbers than they do now—and some ancient invoices from a girl's boarding school. Were those poor girls held captive in this dusty space by some cruel headmistress, perhaps for missing the correct spelling of *Megalosaurus?*

These are the thoughts that raced through our minds, along with our hearts, as we tore from floor to floor...again...*hypothetically*.

The house was 3 floors including additional living space in the attic, with at least two wings, so we could spread out and go off on our own adventures until, eventually, we'd stumble upon one another, sneaking around *this* corner or jumping out of *that* crawlspace over the hall. Usually a conspiracy would be hatched by a few to scare the many...which always succeeded, even when we knew it was coming.

And while the others were content to run from room to room, I would often just wander and breathe in the past.

Perched by a large second floor window I imagined myself Gatsby and took in a large party of flappers and scoundrels making merry on my finely manicured lawn.

Bedrooms hosted house guests warmed by cozy fireplaces.

Below, the main hall was alive with music and light as elegantly dressed women and men mingled and danced, while tuxedoed servants offered canopies and drinks from silver trays, then silently disappeared back into the walls.

Imagination?

Yeah...I guess. I do have a pretty good one.

But when I have these sensations it feels like something so much more. Like looking through the veil of the present, right into the past.

As it turned out, I learned some years later, the old mansion was just that: the home of a rich local benefactor who along with his wife willed the estate to the Town to be used as a public space upon their deaths. The period of decline that we so enjoyed was the transition period in between the time the widow vacated the premises and the time the town took over sometime in the 70's, restored the mansion to its former glory and created a park for all to enjoy. I even played softball on a field situated not 100 yards from the place whose deserted nooks and crannies I once roamed and explored.

Today the mansion is used for weddings and other such events, and yes, I believe they serve canopies and cocktails from silver trays while music fills the halls.

So maybe I wasn't looking back into the past after all. Maybe it was really the future...or more likely a little bit of both

As it turned out, even though it's the house that still haunts my memory, from time to time...it really wasn't a haunted house at all.

It was more a place of happiness and joy, waiting to be reborn.

It just had to make do with our brand of joy, in the meantime...but I don't think it minded at all.

Pre-Vacation Day...

Today is pre-vacation day.

The worst of all days.

We're heading out for a week at the Jersey shore tomorrow.

Z usually takes the day before we leave off and, well, you can guess the rest.

The first thing is to prepare a list of all the lists that need to be made.

The second thing is to adhere to the lists and check completed things off the list as we go. If items are attended to that were not previously on the list, they are added to the list...and then checked off...the list.

Of course packing is a big item on the list. There's all sorts of packing. There's food packing. Food preparation packing. Beverage packing, both non and non-non-alcoholic. There's entertainment packing, which has become much more manageable with the advent of the IPod and or smart-ass phone. No more lugging around 500 CDs just in case you feel moved to play "*Lime in the Coconut*" one night.

There's linen and towel packing, pillow packing, shoe packing, sundry packing, mondry packing and tuesdray packing, as well. Snack packing, which is in addition to food packing, book packing and of course, clothes packing, which most definitely includes bathing suits and towels, since we're going to the beach for a week.

Don't laugh...it's been known to happen; but not with us...not with the list...no way!

Once the lists have been scrutinized and check assured, car packing can now commence. The car is carefully backed down the driveway so the packing materials can be efficiently hauled off the deck and onto the driveway, where the Rubik's cube of packing can begin. You might think that packing a Hyundai with the stuff of two people should be pretty easy, but you would be wrong.

As you know, if you're shore savvy, weather wise, the beach is a funny place. While it may be warm and sunny at 11 AM, it can be cold, windy and cloudy by 4 PM. Therefore one must pack accordingly and pretty much just bring everything they own, including that natty sweater from Aunt Louise.

So there's a lot of stuff

I've actually thought of photographing or diagraming past packing's to expedite things; but I thought that might be excessive. Not to mention weird. Besides, after a while it becomes second nature; until you buy a new car and then you start all over again.

So it's best to keep what you drive as a long as you can. And 1988 was a good year for Hyundais.

Once *ALL* the packing and list checking is completed, a call to our house sitters, Gunter and Gerde, is made to assure them their required supply of lutefisk is in the basement fermenting. We also let them know there's a brand new cushy sofa in the living room for their two very large, very scary, Great Danes, Hans and Feats, to have their way with.

It's nice to know the place will be in good hands while we're away, and the smell of week old lutefisk is always oddly reassuring upon our return.

Before we found Gunter and Gerde, we would just lock everything up tight and take all the usual vacation precautions; stop the mail and the papers, etc.

Z would leave a note behind with our mobile phone numbers, just in case any intruders wanted to get in touch with us; you know, in case they couldn't figure out the remote for the flat screen or where we kept the "good" gin.

Z would also clean the place like a fiend the day before we left and make sure all the trash baskets were empty in the morning. She always claimed it was nice to come home to a clean house. But I always suspected she was really planning ahead in case we became shark food, and she didn't want the "bereaved" relatives who came over to pick through all our stuff to think we had a messy house.

So, with all that in place, we look toward an early morning departure in hopes of beating the incessant traffic on the Parkway.

Best of all, we're now free to hit our pillows, which mostly prevents us from hitting each other.

I mean vacation prep is stressful...list or no lists.

Straddling the Ocean's Edge

Vacations develop a rhythm of their own choosing;

much different than the everyday rhythms we're accustomed to. The sooner you discover that rhythm and begin to step in time to it, the sooner you're able to let yourself go wherever the music wants to take you.

As usual, Z and I found our rhythm in the ebb and flow of the ocean tide as it flowed and ebbed up onto the shore and over our sometimes sandy toes.

A sort of intrinsic internal clock always told us when it was time to head to the beach—mostly early morning, a couple of hours after dawn—where we would park our chairs, spread our towels and stake our umbrellas around a half acre of sand, because we don't like strangers, woozy from the waves, putting their sandy toes on our non-sandy blankets.

We began most every morning in this same way, alone, ahead of the others, then immediately take-off up the beach straddling the ocean's edge; a half hour or so up, and a half hour or so back.

There's a lot to be learned along the ocean's edge, not the least of which is, you can develop an ugly blood blister on your big toe if you're not careful.

At the time, there was apparently a nasty heat wave going on back home, but the magic of the ocean breeze kept all that heat at bay, as it were, especially at that hour of the morning with the sun still reflecting, long off the water.

Anne Morrow Lindbergh wrote a beautiful book back in the 50's called *"Gift from the Sea",* in which she reflects on the various sea shells that are delivered to her spot on the beach every morning. Each item held meaning to her and delivered a message about life and relationships of all kinds...to each other, to nature...even the chatty old man on the nearby blanket that NEVER shut up the entire week.

Z and I are the perfect complimentary beach walking buddies. I have a tendency to look down when I stride, head, who knows where, following the mottled prints of all the beach feet that came before.

Z on the other hand, walks firmly in the present, head held high, savoring the misty ocean air, eyes always alert for hidden treasures.

This year it was dolphins, by the bushel. We've always had occasion to see them throughout our beach weeks in the past, usually a ways a way, off in the distance, generally in sets of two or three.

It's always a big occasion when folks spot them, accompanied by a lot of murmuring and dashes to the shore line.

I don't know how she does it, whether they send her a secret message or not, but Z always seems to be the one who lifts her head and says "*Dolphins!*" in the same manner that Radar O'Reilly would announce the incoming choppers on Mash.

For some reason, this week, the sea was full of them, breaching and playing, swimming around in groups much larger than any we'd ever seen in the past. At one point they had come in so close to the shore, the life guards pulled everyone from the water.

Not sure why...I guess because Dolphins have been known to run off with other people's boogie boards.

At least that was my theory.

Another theory is that Dolphins always arrive with a special message for everyone to whom they present themselves. A lot of people feel it's a sign to slow down, empty your brain and enjoy the simple pleasures. To understand, no matter what insanity the world seem to manufacture at times, we're all the same, existing together, whether on land or in the sea.

That's the message some people receive.

The message I usually receive is, I should slow down, empty my brain and get a cheese steak for lunch.

Don't ask me why, I guess it's just me....

Z says that's a very self-serving message and she doubts the dolphins would make the trip just to deliver my lunch menu.

I just shake my head at her skepticism and say, "*Its Dolphins...who am I to question?*"

We continued on our outbound excursion up the beach for a bit longer, until we hit the two mile mark where we would usually turn around, but noticed we were close to an area of beach reclamation, which was said to be yielding a rare supply of sand dollars, unearthed by the recent dredging.

Z thought we should walk on ahead a little and see if we could pick up a cretaceous buck or two.

Believe it or not, I was the first to come up with one, or half a dollar as it were, or a *"Fity cent"* piece of sea shell.

Of course Z went on to find several others, intact, yet on the small side, but the point was, it was a rare find, and anything rare is always welcome...including my impending cheese steak.

After an unplanned bit of sea shell hunting we finally turned around, mindful of the extra mile and a half we added on to our journey and walked back along the familiar shoreline. This time we had the benefit of the cool breeze in our faces, which was a refreshing treat. However, cool breeze aside, what was also different was the much larger, solitary, shadowy shape, barely breaching the waves in front of us.

At the same moment, a group of life guards, gathered for their morning roster call, all turned at once and began to point towards the ocean. This was obviously not your average Dolphin sighting.

Then a bit further to the south of our first glimpse, a long, majestic streak of shiny black rolled gracefully from the water, then slipped back beneath the waves. It was a whale...something we had never seen there before, and something so obviously rare, especially this close, even the life guards were excited by it.

Z and I just stood there; mouths open, marveling at what we had just seen. It also struck us that if we had not walked the extra distance to gather the sand dollars, we would probably never have seen it at all.

I asked Z what message she thought THAT was supposed to be? She just shrugged and said she wasn't sure, but maybe there *was* real value in finding those sand dollars, after all.

I, on the other hand had no doubt, what special message the whale was sending to me...it was telling me..."*Go for the cheesy fries, as well!*"

Which I did....

This all took place on a Tuesday, but it really defined and highlighted the rest of our week, which also included a day of swimming with the Rays, always a treat. Of course there were several nice dinners out—one in which a passing waiter spilled a mug of beer on me as I was leaving my name at the desk, which resulted in my scoring a t-shirt plus a trip to the head of a hungry line of diners for my soggy troubles—many trips for ice cream and gelato, shopping and all the other things you do on a vacation.

By Thursday some cloudy, breezy weather rolled into town and by Friday we were entrenched under a blanket of rain, wind and end of vacation blues.

But now that I'm home, back clacking away, it seems clear, the gift left behind on that special day of dolphins, sand dollars and whales was, and will be, a lasting one....

Keep your head up, eyes focused and mind open.

But most importantly, always look to the sea...and straddle the ocean's edge every chance you get.

Dandelion Discourse

There are a lot of Dandelions this year...a lot.

Those little yellow headed critters that dot our lawns all spring and summer.

Well, not mine...at least not for long. Let's just say, they know better than to make a stop on my lawn.

My grandmother used to eat dandelions, which embarrassed the rest of us. I mean she could have put them on a plate...or at least picked them out of the grass first.

No...I'm kidding. It's not like she was some kind of granny goat. She'd trudge around the yard, in the dress she always wore instead of pants, and cut them down with a knife. Then she'd clean them up and make a salad out of them. I was the only other person in the family that actually liked them. A little bitter, if I recall, but hey, so am I, so it suited me.

I actually saw my first dandelion pop up as early as February, this year. They're resilient little guys and you have to admire that.

They just don't get their due, at least as far as flowers go. In fact, I bet most of you just call them weeds.

Yeah...me too, until I found out the hard way; there's a lot more to them than that.

I was out the other day; let's say "dealing" with said dandelions, when one of them starts to chat me up.

I hate that.

Especially when...you know...I have plans for them.

I mean do I really need to assign a face to my dandelions?

Anyway, this dandelion tells me that being a dandelion in this century blows.

That once they were held in very high regard; even given the name of "Lion's Tooth" to distinguish them from all the other pedestrian vegetation out there.

Now, everyone just sees them as weeds, which they find insulting. No one sees them for what they are, which, as I said, is really just a flower...a flower like any other kind of flower.

"Well," I said to the dandelion, "these days folks like to keep their lawns nice and green. In fact they spend a lot of money on it. You guys sort of muck that up with all that yellow."

"So, what's wrong with yellow? There are yellow tulips, carnations, daisies...and what about that obnoxious yellow rose of Texas, who thinks so highly of himself just because someone wrote a song about him? No one complains about any of them!"

Things were starting to get a little heated now, at least from the dandelion's perspective, so I thought I'd better try to smooth things over a bit. You don't want to get a dandelion all worked up. It can take hours to calm them down, once you do.

"Listen, ah...Dan...can I call you Dan?"

"Why would you call me Dan? My name's Greg...."

"Oh...sorry...I just assumed—"

"Of course you just assumed....*EVERYBODY* just assumes, when it comes to the dopey dandelions!"

"Okay calm down...."

"Calm down? Why should I calm down? Don't you think I know what you're up to with that little spray bottle you're hiding behind your back?"

"Well, no. I—"

"I bet you don't know about our medicinal properties? Or all the nutrients we put back into the soil to make your precious little graminoids flourish.

"My what?"

'You're lawn, idiot!"

"Oh...."

"We're good for all kinds of things...we even make a tasty salad...just ask your grandmother."

"You knew my grandmother? But how...?"

"What...you think this measly little week is all I get? Hey buddy, wise up. You know all those little puffy seeds you used to blow on when you were a kid?"

"Yeah...."

"Well, just more of me, cloning myself over and over again, year after year, decade after decade. But one little squirt from your bottle of poison there and that's the end of that."

"But that's the problem", I said, now armed with a salient point. "You just scatter to the wind and spread your seed everywhere...there's no end to where you'll pop up."

"Hey, what do you expect...I'm French," he replied with a wink.

"Alright," I said. "You make some good points. I was really just coming out here to deal with the clover."

"Good idea...they never *were* lucky, anyway. And take care of that Chickweed and Creeping Charlie, while you're at it. They're nothing but a bunch of hooligans that give us all a bad name."

And so I did.

When I returned a few days later, Greg had already transformed into a little, white puff ball of seed.

Gently, I picked him up from his little patch of earth and recalled our conversation.

Then, I proceeded to blow, gently...all over my neighbor's lawn.

I don't need any more obnoxious little know it all dandelions on mine....

Literary Road Trip

Midweek of our "Staycation" found us, curiously enough, "*not staying*" but instead opting for a brief road trip up north to the land of revolution, enlightenment...and the bar where everyone knows your name.

That's right, the great "*Commonwealth*" of Massachusetts, which I dare you to spell without using spell check.

Notice I said "*Commonwealth*" of Massachusetts, which is basically a hoity toity way of saying state. But what else would you expect from a place that burned women for entertainment, essentially because they were suffering severe symptoms of extreme PMS. But in all fairness, that was a while ago, and when you think about it....

Massachusetts is also the home of the once, long suffering Red Sox fan, who up until 2004, had not seen their team win the World Series since about 1776, when there was only one other team in the league, who happened to be British and found it difficult to run the bases without losing their powdered wigs.

We decided to take a quick trip to old Sturbridge Village to essentially go back in time to the early 19th century, but with a stopover in Concord, home of the famous grape jelly. It's also the town where the *"shot heard round the world"* occurred at the old north bridge marking the first official battle of the American Revolution, which you may have heard about.

Concord also boasts having been the onetime home to several of the most notable American authors of their time, or any time....all at one time.

Ralph Waldo Emerson, of whom Thoreau was attributed to have said, **"He's a pretty cool dude, for an old guy..."**, was noted for advancing the Transcendentalism movement, which I believe had something to do with molar replacement....

The aforementioned Henry David Thoreau, the famed naturalist who also wrote:

> **"I went to the woods because I wished to live deliberately, to front only the essential facts of life, and see if I could not learn what it had to teach, and not, when I came to die, discover that I had not lived....in New Jersey."**

Nathaniel Hawthorne, who had a thing for big red letters and houses with funky roof lines. He was generally considered to be an old stick in the mud, and is said to have written the now famous axiom:

> **"I like brown...it suits me...."**

And last but not least, Louisa May Alcott, noted abolitionist, best known for her novel *"Little Women"*.

Ms. Alcott cherished her role as an independent woman and wrote:

> ..."*though not an easy life, it is a free one, and I enjoy it. I can't do much with my hands; so I will make a battering-ram of my head and make a way through this rough-and-tumble world...without coupons.*"

Unfortunately our GPS guide, Michelle, who to be honest, because of her pushiness, was not the most personable of travel companions, mixed up the coordinates and initially sent us to Concord's lesser known sister town, Skippy, MA... home of the popular peanut butter, the old south bridge, famous for nothing, other than it hasn't collapsed in the last several months and an assemblage of some of 19th Century America's dimmer intellectual lights.

Where's Waldo Emerson, Ralph's 2nd cousin, best known for his garish, striped shirts, silly wool hat, and a propensity for hiding in large crowds.

Herman Thoreau, said to be, but never verified, Henry's 3rd cousin, twice removed, once by the authorities and once by his wife, who, instead of going to the woods to live, went to the sea, where he subsequently drowned in the first few minutes and therefore never wrote anything of consequence.

Daniel Hawthorne, no relation to Nathaniel, who was sent to prison for spray painting graffiti on women's chests, and Louie Alcott, Louise's deranged Uncle from Philadelphia who began a novel called "*Little Thumbs and Toes*" but never finished it once he heard that another author in New York had beat him to the punch by publishing a similarly themed book entitled" *Little Pinkies and Knees*".

Eventually, we were able to convince Michelle, she had led us to the wrong "*destination*" as she likes to say, and after a series of snide "*recalculating routes*" we soon found ourselves at the Concord museum, although she stubbornly refused to admit making a mistake.

It was actually kind of cool walking through all the exhibits, seeing Thoreau's old furniture and Emerson's study; imagining, hanging out in there with all of them, shooting the breeze...despite the scarcity of indoor plumbing.

In a way, they were all just early day bloggers...with bad hair.

They wrote essays on unique topics, sharing distinctive insights such as man's relationship with nature as a way of connecting to the whole; all the mysteries of the universe and beyond answered in a single drop of rain falling in a pond.

Emerson declared "*literary independence*" in the United States and urged Americans to create a writing style all their own, free from European influences, paving the way for a revolution in writing that unveiled the true face and voice of America, a country endlessly in transition.

And Thoreau with his urge to simplify, perceiving the world through an army of ant's battling it out on his window sill, on a lazy afternoon.

Or professing the futility of labor at the expense of the soul...and making you smile about it all, to boot.

Of Thoreau, Emerson wrote:

"My good Henry Thoreau made this else solitary afternoon sunny with his simplicity & clear perception. How comic is simplicity in this double-dealing quacking world. Everything that boy says makes merry with society though nothing can be graver than his meaning".

Hmmmmm...kind of makes me look at this whole blogging thing in a whole new light.

I wonder where they'll put the gift shop....?

Thoroughly Thoreau

Last time, I was relating the tale of our visit to

Concord and all the great authors that once lived there. Now, they're actually all buried there as well, high up on a ridge that requires a billy goat and a Sherpa to access.

It's a nice little tourist attraction, featured on all the visitor maps, although on the day we were there we had the place all to ourselves. Very bucolic as cemeteries go, populated with both the long dead and the newly dead, eternally resting, side by side.

They even named the place, Author's Ridge, in honor of the famous scribblers, but I understand that's a point of contention with some of the non-literati among the reposed.

What strikes you as you view these antiquated graves of those who, in life, stood out in such a notable manner, is how simple and unadorned they are, surrounded by generations of family members. In fact if you weren't carrying a map, you'd pass them by entirely.

It's interesting to note, in a melancholic sort of way, except for Emerson, who lived to be nearly 79, they all died before 60; Thoreau the youngest at 44. I guess that was not uncommon for those times since pretty much anything from the flu to a cut finger could kill you, but it kind of puts things into perspective when, even at a few years short of 60, we feel as if we can expect another 60.

Aside from Emerson's granite boulder of a tombstone, all the others markers are pretty non-descript. I like Thoreau's the best wherein keeping with his *simplify, simplify,* philosophy, it merely says "*Henry*".

It's a tradition, for some folks, I guess, to carry up stones and twigs and place them on a loved one's final resting place. But it's pretty easy to pick out the Author's markers by the odd assortment of pens, note paper and reading glasses that garnish them...even an assortment of M&M's.

Well, the M&M's were mine and fell out of my pocket when I leaned over to pick up a snazzy Montblanc someone had left for Louisa May.

Z just gave me that look she's perfected through the years and made me put it back; all without saying a word.

So I took back my M&M's...just for spite.

Then it was on to a more lively setting by way of Walden Pond.

Walden of course is the place where Thoreau built his little house in the woods.

Most people think of a little rustic shack when they think of Thoreau's digs, but they were far from that. In fact, a place like that today would fetch at least $1,200 a week down at the shore.

I've always felt a connection to Henry David—formerly David Henry...no kidding—ever since I read Walden about 20 plus years ago. There's just something about the easy going way he breaks the whole of life down to basics.

Eat, sleep and...well, I'll let you fill in the rest.

Okay I'll say it....

Observe....

Observe and make note of everything around you. Everything that defines you...cuz it's all there in front of you...*if you open your eyes*.

Plus he frowned on heavy labor, a concept with which most freelance writers would concur.

I've been to Walden a few times over the years, but first time visitors are always a little surprised to see that it's actually a state park or reservation now, plus a popular beach destination, complete with snack bar, beach chairs and all the rest. The same as any beach.

As you take a walk around the pond's perimeter, you find quite a few more adventurous types, setting up in little nooks and crannies; diving into crystal, blue water; little glints of sun dancing back to the shore.

Soon you approach the farthest northeast corner, and up on a hill, overlooking the pond, now somewhat hidden by thickets of trees, is the old foundation of Thoreau's little one room house.

When I first stepped into that little granite rectangle of standing stones that mark the site, some 15 years or so ago, I immediately felt something stir in me....and I knew it wasn't the leftover tacos we had brought from home, but left in the car.

The woods were overcast with clouds that day and I was alone, since Z had decided to take a little snooze after lunch on the small beach below.

So I set up my camera on one of the stones across the way and put it on a timer.

As the clock ticked down, I hurried to position myself, and leaned against the standing stone that marked where the front door would have been. If you've ever taken one of these self-portraits, you know you hurry to get set, then don't know what to do with yourself as you wait for the shutter to click; all the while wondering if you even set the timer correctly.

As I stood there, for some reason I folded my arms across my chest and was just about to abandon the effort when suddenly the sun broke through the clouds and streamed in through the trees, lighting on my face. Just then, I heard the camera click and the shot was taken, leaving behind an ethereal photo that evoked the strange sensation I had been feeling inside.

Quite a few years later, we returned to Walden, and while browsing through the gift shop I came across a simple drawing of Thoreau standing at the doorway of his cabin, arms folded, another gentle light upon his face.

Now, I know it's just an artist's drawing, but I found the coincidence to be very, very cool.

Today, both pictures hang on my office wall; the writing factory as it were.

Just a reminder, at least to me, that the things that resonate, resonate for a reason and should not be lightly dismissed.

Thoreau said it best...*of course*....

"If a man loses pace with his companions, perhaps it is because he hears a different drummer. Let him step to the music which he hears, however measured, or far away."

High on Higgs Boson

A bunch of physicists got together in Geneva

Switzerland on the 4th of July to announce they've discovered something called "The God Particle", which had been theorized to exist for a while now, but never proved.

A little like my ex college roommate's supposed girlfriend.

This announcement led to a lot of excitement and applause among the scientist that had gathered there, along with numerous reported incidences of raucous physicist behavior including the unprotected exchange of pocket protectors.

The rest of us just went..."*Huh...?*"

But the rest of us can't even spell "*physicist*" without the help of spellcheck.

In fact some of us can't even spell "*spellcheck*" without the help of spellcheck.

Apparently this "God Particle", a name, by the way, the scientist don't like to use—they like to use the official signifier "Higgs Boson"—is the thing that showed up shortly after the "Big Bang" that gave matter mass, which gave it weight, which led to the creation of large round spheres.

I guess kind of like those dozen brownies I consumed the other night...with the bowl of vanilla Häagen-Dazs ...and Hershey's, which led to another large round sphere above my waist.

So why do I need a bunch of egg heads to spend a lot of money to tell me why I get fat?

Isn't it bad enough that I do?

But I guess that's the way of the world...or the universe or...something.

What may not be of any matter to you and me, is certainly a big bunch of matter to others...especially if they have a microscope.

Actually, what they have is this 10 billion dollar big giant 17 mile long tunnel like tube thing called the Large Hadron Collider or what the scientist like to call the LHC, which, to be honest, isn't a very creative nickname considering it cost 10 billion dollars.

Anyway, this so called LHC is the world's largest particle accelerator—way bigger than the one Wal-Mart sells for $29.95—and is located deep beneath the Swiss Alps.

It was originally scheduled to be turned on a couple of years ago, when a lot of theories abounded that in doing so, scientists risked destroying the very fabric of the universe by possibly creating an all-encompassing black hole that some speculated would swallow everything in the cosmos, leaving behind a vacuum of, well, nothingness.

Of course the physicists scoffed at this notion and said it was something like a 99.9% *unlikelihood* that anything would happen along those lines...so they decided to go for it....despite the 00.1% that it could.

What's a little non-existence between scientists?

Unfortunately—or fortunately—almost immediately after they turned the thing on it blew a fuse of something and shut down; the odds of which were something like 100% unlikely to happen.

But it did and nobody had another fuse, so the whole program was put on hold until some guy named Hans could find a hardware store that carried fuses for the world's largest particle accelerator.

Luckily, other than some embarrassed scientific egos, no damage or other untoward events were reported, other than the disappearance of a group of Swiss Yodelers, who were holding their annual convention at a nearby resort.

Bygones....

A year or so later, Hans returned with the new fuse and the Collider started colliding and smashing all manner of photons and protons, much to the relief of the gathered researchers, not to mention the rest of us, as no cataclysmic black holes were reported, other than the sudden rise in popularity of the singer, Adele.

And now, some 18 months after that, these giddy physicists say they believe they've discovered...or are pretty sure they've discovered the Higgs Boson, or "God Particle"...at least, with a "high degree of certainty", 99.9% sure.

According to a report on "Yahoo News", which seems like the appropriate news outlet for this story....

"The scientists did not spot the particle per se but detected its footprint when observing high-speed collisions of other subatomic particles in two separate experiments conducted with the ATLAS and CMS

particle-collision detectors, which detect collisions within CERN's Large Hadron Collider."

Which to me sounds an awful lot like some guy in the mountains saying he didn't actually see "Bigfoot" in them there woods, but detected its footprint in the snow while exploring the bottom of a bottle of homemade hooch.

I don't mean to sound like some kind of skeptic here—okay, maybe I do...a little—but when it comes to my "God Particles" I kind of want a little better rate of certainty than that.

Don't you?

If we're going to all the trouble of unlocking the secrets of the Universe I want to be pretty darn certain we're unlocking the right ones.

Does anyone *not* remember that Star Trek episode with the Tribbles?

Besides...what's it matter...what the matter?

It's like saying, *"I know where water comes from."*

Good for you...but is it really worth billions of dollars?

It's there...it's wet...it's cool...just drink it.

Matter or no matter....

Mass...or no *más* ....

Who knows?

Certainly not me.

Maybe someday it will lead to free cable.

But for 10 billion dollars maybe we can cover that last 0.1%.

Can't be too careful.

You know...?

Gotta Love the Zen

My brains' acting out.

It's pouting and grumbling, refusing to give me any ideas to write about today. So, I thought this would be a good time to bring up Zen.

I love Zen.

Zen is the Seinfeld of spiritual philosophies and disciplines.

Zen, in its purist form, its only form, is about *nothing*.

And that's perfect for me....

I can do nothing...with my eyes closed.

This is my favorite unattributed Zen saying:

"To know that there is nothing to know,
And to grieve that it is so difficult
to communicate this "nothing to know" to others—
this is the life of Zen,
this is the deepest thing in the world...."

How cool is that!

I've been trying to tell people that exact same thing for years, except my method involves a lot shouting, disdainful looks and hair pulling...sometimes theirs.

And the beauty of Zen is the less you know, the more you know....

You know?

And that's alright with me. Especially since my brain is on a time out.

There's a Zen sign called the "open circle". There's another symbol called the "closed circle", but we're not discussing that today...because I say so.

From Energy Healing Circle.com_:

"The open circle represents the imperfection found in all things, and suggests to the student to stop striving for perfection and instead to allow the universe to be as it is."

See...just like I was trying to tell them in High School!

"The open circle is a concept that reflects closely with Japanese Zen Buddhism. The Japanese concept of wabi sabi is that all things are perfect as they are..."

So there!

An example would be, someone collecting banana shaped stones on the beach, any beach. But instead of scouring the beach, day after day, wreaking havoc on their C2 vertebrae, they could easily go out and buy dozens of banana shaped stones in a store, someplace, and each one would be shiny, bright and perfect.

But they don't...cuz to the Zenster, these manufactured stones could never equal the *perfection* found in the *imperfection* of the real banana shaped stones hiding beneath the muddy shore. Plus, in a way, aren't the stones really finding you, instead of you finding them?

Capice?

And that's so cool. That's so Zen....

Buying them in a store is just so retail...unless they're on sale.

And if that doesn't make any sense to you, then more the better. It's Zen!

Anyway gotta go. My brain is starting to quibble with my body again. I've gotta separate them.

But I'll leave you with this, a quote from the Buddha himself:

"People with opinions just go around bothering one another...."

Gotta love the Zen...

What Happened to the Future?

What happened to the future?

I mean the future everyone was talking about when I was a kid back in the 60's.

The one where we all lived propped up on mile high towers in near-space where the stars shone all the time. We drove, or flew rather, on skyways in tiny little space cars enclosed with synthetic see through bubble tops.

Hi-tech machines and robots took care of all of our menial chores, including bathing, brushing our teeth and even dressing us. All you need do was push a few buttons and off you went down a conveyor belt and into some sort of electronic phone booth where, within seconds, you emerged from the other side fully clothed and ready for your day at the sprocket factory...but not before saying goodbye to Jane your wife...daughter Judy and your boy, Elroy.

What happened to that future with all the cool toys that were promised, like wall size 3D holographic interactive TVs, indoor dog walkers and robots named Rosie to keep your sky pad up and running in tip top button pushing shape?

When I was a kid I couldn't wait for that future. It might have been the cool, high collared stretchy outfits, but I think it was more the idea that anything imagined was possible or within reach of possible, through technology...although I had never heard or used the word technology, back then. Back then, the most technology I came in contact with was the transistor radio I could sneak into the classroom to listen to the World Series through a tiny earphone that used to belong to Marconi. And I guess there were my glow in the dark monster toys. But they only glowed for about 10 seconds and I think sent radioactive ions into my frontal lobe...I think.

So certain and anxious was I for this brave new world, that I actually counted off the years until we reached this utopian space age, which I associated with the year 2000. I was about 8 at the time, in 1962, so 38 more years to go was the magic number. But my anticipatory enthusiasm was a little bittersweet because I also calculated that I would be all of 46 by then, pretty old to fully enjoy it all.

But hey, maybe in the future 46 wouldn't be all that old. Maybe 46 would be the new 18!

The NY World's Fair came along in 1964 and reinforced all my expectations. Futuristic towers and buildings as far as the eye could see. Gleaming monorails streaking overhead. Cars that drove on streets AND water. Moving sidewalks and huge waffles with strawberries and whip cream...the food of the 21st century, right there for the taking.

At the Bell Telephone pavilion they said we would all be using picture phones by 1970, and while that was slightly more than half a lifetime for an overly imaginative 10 year old, it seemed doable...but just barely.

The GM pavilion had it all. Tall space needle buildings, flying cars...even underwater cities.

They even had this scary round machine that we all gathered around and watched as they split an atom or something, creating this loud intense boom. This I assumed, in my decade old brain, was the boom that would jettison us up into our little space apartments and cars. It was all making sense...at least to me.

Vacationing on the moon...hiking on Mars....

This was happening people!

Only it didn't....

Oh sure...we do have microwave ovens that can cook a chicken in about 10 seconds. But did you ever eat a microwaved chicken?

We have a lifetime of collected music on devices the size of a stick of gum.

Mobile phones and computers that can tell us anything we need to know...except how to get to grandma's house without going over the river and through the woods.

Flat screen TV's that can fill an entire wall.

Medical imaging that can spot a pin hole on your liver.

Digital space pictures of Uranus as clear as...well, let's leave that to the imagination.

We have all that and more, but it doesn't seem like enough.

I guess the future loses some of its shine when it becomes the present.

We still have all the bad stuff that we had hoped would disappear. And in some cases the bad stuff seems worse than ever. Far from the Utopia we were lead to believe was on the way.

On top of all that....no flying cars, no spaceways, no robots to clean the toilet...not even the cool high collared stretchy suits.

Basically, I'm still wearing the same old clothes I wore in the 60's....

Even my cool futuristic World's Fair hat.

Just try taking that away from me....

Narcissistic Nitwit

The bad thing about being a Narcissistic Nitwit is—A: you were probably born a Narcissistic Nitwit, and B: you will probably always be a Narcissistic Nitwit.

The good thing is, since you *are* a Narcissistic Nitwit—A: you don't mind being a Narcissistic Nitwit, and B: you eventually come to think that being a Narcissistic Nitwit is the greatest thing in the world...if you hadn't already...which you probably had.

Having said that, I guess one of the nicer things—Narcissistic Nitwit or not—about sitting where I sit nowadays, is I'm able to see the world from both sides of the fence.

Plus I can use confusing double metaphors, which nobody really understands, but won't question, because they figure I'm old enough and experienced enough that it must mean *something*... which isn't necessarily true.

But in this case it is.

What I'm suggesting, or pontificating—which is more accurate—is, when you're young and coming into your own, you basically think you understand everything there is to know about the universe, in all its grand majesty...plus a couple of other universes that most people aren't even aware exist.

You feel, once you learned to ride a bike, you also invented the wheel...and the little bell thingie.

And now you can't wait to tell other people about it.

In fact you can't imagine how the world has been able to manage without this wheel—let alone the little bell thingie—for so long, in the first place.

But you're more than happy to share your unique perspectives and insights with all the clueless unfortunates in the world, whose lives you are more than happy to enhance.

Thank me...thank me very much....

I'm more than welcome...yes, I know, I know....

No need to embarrass yourself. Let me....

Then after you live a while—actually *live* and experience all the sides and all the angles life has to offer, the light, the shadows and those murky areas in between—you realize nobody, least of all you, has all the answers.

And boy, let me tell you...*is that ever a relief!*

I mean who needs all that responsibility?

Not a Narcissistic Nitwit like me....

Sure, it's natural, once you get a little age under your belt, to have an inclination to help others in avoiding the same mistakes that you made. So you can't resist offering a little grey beard advice now and again.

And once you do, whether or not it's heeded isn't really your concern. It's enough that you put it out there.

And, the truth is, we *know* the lessons best learned were the ones we taught ourselves by making those mistakes in the first place.

And when we fell, we had a choice: sit there and feel sorry for ourselves, hoping someone will come and bail us out...or pick ourselves up and try not to make the same mistake twice.

I usually took the latter approach, mostly because I was too much of a Narcissistic Nitwit to take no for an answer. And because I was a Narcissistic Nitwit, I usually made the same mistake more than twice...with the same results, which is also the definition by some—not me—of crazy.

But the world needs the Narcissistic Nitwit. Without them we probably wouldn't have a light bulb, or a computer, or an iPod. We also probably wouldn't have a couple of dozen buildings and golf courses named Trump, but hey...nobody said it was a perfect system.

I mean no one asked *ME* to design it....

Unfortunately, for every successful Narcissistic Nitwit there are probably ten thousand unsuccessful ones, who basically can't get out of their own way. But they're not hurting anyone, other than themselves...and their families...and their friends...and their coworkers...and every poor person in the world who has to offer them a service of some sort or another *and just don't know what they're doing!!!!!*

But I digress....

As I said...it gets better with age. Presbyopia aside, you begin to see things a lot clearer the further you move away from your overextended goals.

You start to realize, where you *are* is really not too bad, and the way you got there, circuitous or not, was the way you *needed* to go.

And you see the same is true for everyone around you.

They didn't need to do it the way you thought they needed to do it, when you were young; the way you did or didn't do it. The way you suddenly discovered and *knew* would save the world.

Now, you understand; they already knew it and discarded it. Knew it wasn't for them, much to your disdain and condescending contempt and loathing.

That's just the way of the world.

Why should you waste all your genius and greatness on them?

And if you're not smart enough to know that...well, then, I just feel sorry for you....

AM I JUST WASTING MY BREATH HERE PEOPLE!!!!!!!

Jaunting in July

July is an all business kind of month; one of only two full

months of summer, really...at least officially.

July is when all the schools are closed and the pools and beaches are open.

July hosts the 4th of July, which is fortuitous, and is the first real vacation month where people close their computers, walk away from their spread sheets and pack up their families and or themselves and head off to their vacation destination of choice.

Today, people go to all sorts of vacation destinations.

There are beach people, mountain people, 110 degree Florida theme park people.

Resort people, camping people...all kinds of people....all on vacation.

It was a bit different when I was a kid.

When I was a kid, a jaunt to the local beach was considered a vacation...but only if my dad came along, and only if it occurred in the middle of the week.

If I was just with my mom or it was a Saturday or Sunday, then it wasn't a vacation at all...just business as usual.

Every once in a while though we did get to go on a *"real"* vacation, which consisted of all of us piling into our old, but reliable, Chevy and accompanying my dad on a business trip to Canajoharie, NY, where he periodically dropped in on the Beechnut Life Saver and Gum factory to take care of some pressing candy business or another.

Not sure what he actually did there, but I like to imagine it had something to do with peppermint.

While my dad went off to work, the rest of us got to hang out at the pool at the Thruway Motel in nearby Albany.

I know it doesn't sound like much, now, but it was a very advanced pool. It had a very cool water slide, which was about all of nine feet long and...wait for it...an actual diving board.

I know....

What more could a kid want.

Who needs waves, tall pines or big eared mouse men to entertain?

And if we were good, at lunch time my mom would order us...again, wait for it...this exotic sandwich called a *Turkey Club*, which had three slices of toasted bread, and was cut into quarters, the way they did it on tropical islands...at least according to my mom.

In the evening, after another tasty meal at the Thruway Cantina, we would saunter across the parking lot to the new Cinerama movie theatre where we would catch the latest summer blockbuster, featuring a cast of thousand, most notably *"How the*

West Was Won", which seemed to always be playing, and was literally about 3 hours long.

I know....

Hard to imagine how great it really was. And the Albany popcorn was so much better than your everyday popcorn, for some reason.

By the next day, of course, we were all vacationed out—I mean how much can a person take—so we piled back into the Chevy, barely able to hold our heads up and motored south, back down the Thruway, from whence we came, towards home. A reluctant return to the summer reality of prickly heat afternoons and firefly catching and enslaving nights.

I guess compared to today, it really wasn't much. But it was what we had, and it must have been something...cuz I'm still thinking about it today.

I'm a Met fan!

I'm a Met fan! I'm not ashamed to say it.

I'm a Met fan!

There I said it again....

It's not like it's my choice.

No...there's no choice involved.

Who would choose to go through what a Met fan goes through in a lifetime?

No...it's not a choice. It's a way of life. It's who we are; how we were born.

It's genetically pre-determined.

Like other traits that wrap around our DNA: loyalty, truthfulness, trustfulness, kindness, grumpiness, pragmatist, fatalist, pessimist...even how we tie our shoes.

None of it's our choice; it's just who we are.

For those of my particular generation, we've been there from the beginning, since 1962.

Witnesses to the birth of a team...even if we were really too young to appreciate what that meant at the time.

Much too young to know, let alone understand, anything about Brooklyn Dodgers or NY Giants.

Only that our dads, and sometimes moms, were rabid fans of either one or the other...never both. Impossible to root for both. Not a "real fan". Not even if they were playing the Yankees in the "series". Not even then.

Then they would withdraw from this world, take a trip to China, Pogo Pogo, even Mars for as long as it took for the nightmare to be over, and the world to right itself again.

I began to come of baseball age around 1961. And if you're a baseball enthusiast you know what that means.

The M & M boys, battling it out for the Home Run title. To Bust the Babe, as it were on the march to 61 homers.

In 61, the Yankees were the only game in town, and not that I was really all that interested, but a lot of the older kids were and I thought I'd better be too.

One day I actually snuck out to the car, so my dad wouldn't know of the sacrilege about to unfold, and turned on the radio to listen to a game...a frickin *Yankee* game!

If you have a good imagination, like I have, listening to a baseball game—any baseball game—on the radio is the greatest experience in the world. There was, of course, Mel Allen, with his Alabama twang, announcing Ballantine blasts, the roar of the crowd, bats knocking on balls, even the sound of the peanut guys yelling, *"Peanuts here! Get your fresh roasted peanuts here!"* and back then, they *were* fresh roasted.

Suddenly, the driver side door springs open and there is my dad....

"What are you doing?

"Nothing."

"Doesn't look like nothing."

The expression on his face was as if he had found me in the back seat with a fifth of scotch, smoking cigars...and I hadn't offered him any.

"I was just...listening to see if Mickey Mantle hit another homer.

"Mantles a bum. Willie runs circles around Mantle...that bum!"

Which struck me as very odd since I didn't think that was part of the game, or else I hadn't heard of it until then, this circle running around.

"Well, I'm really rooting for Maris."

"Maris is a communist!"

"Oh...."

I was pretty sure he wasn't. Though I had no idea what a communist was other than they liked all things pink.

"Next year, real baseball comes back to New York. Next year we have a brand new team to root for ...the Mets!"

"What's a met?"

An honest question, I thought. I knew what a Yankee was, a Pirate, a Giant, A Tiger....

What the heck was a met?

"It stands for Metropolitans, which means people who live in the city. And New York is the most famous city in the world so...."

"The Mets," I finished.

"Yep, and they'll wear blue like the Dodgers, the real bums, and orange like the Giants...and pinstripes like the Yankees", he added reluctantly.

"Oh yeah...pinstripes?"

And so in 1962 the Mets were born, and so was my life as a Met fan, whether I wanted it or not. Again...it wasn't a choice.

In those very early years, we spent, my dad and I, countless summer nights, sitting on the front porch with our old black & white 19 inch portable TV propped up next to the window screen, listening to Bob and Ralph and Lindsey.

There was a funny old man in a baggy uniform who spoke in a language all his own. The players, mostly old Giants and Dodgers, well past their prime, would hit and field, mostly like other teams, except rarely did they win.

My dad had a bunch of homemade score sheets printed up and taught me how to keep score, mostly so I would pay attention, instead of counting the number of chocolate chips in my cookies.

Like I said, they rarely won, but when they did, like on the sticky humid night in August when a skinny, jug eared guy named Jim Hickman...number 9, stepped up to the plate with 2 outs in the bottom of the ninth, worked a 3-2 count, then hit a game winning home run, just barely, into the left field stands of the Polo Grounds, that broke newly numbered 13, Roger Craig's 4 million game losing streak, it felt as if we had won the world series, all in that one game!

And my first time in that ancient, narrow horseshoe of a place called "The Polo Grounds"—for no reason other than it always was—sitting in the first row, field level, directly behind 3rd base, I witnessed a very "grey" 36 year old Duke Snyder leg out a triple, slide in to 3rd and pop up huffing and puffing as if he had just run a marathon. We sat close enough that the cloud of infield dust that Duke had kicked up, settled on our clothes, and I could see every line of sweat, that dripped from his weathered face, onto his uniform.

And that uniform...I will never forget the brightness of the Duke's royal blue sleeves and Orange trim around that shiny satin "*METS*" heaving across his chest.

And after the game—I had no idea if we won or lost, but you could probably guess—they opened up the gates, and actually let us run onto the field, stand on 2nd base and marvel at the breadth and height of the stands rising all around.

Shortly after the start of the 1967 season, the front porch, summer nights came to a sudden end. My dad never got to see the magic of 69 or dominance of 86...I watched those on my own. He never got to experience the absolute joy of all those nickel losses finally turned to gold.

The sublime magic, enhanced by the rarity itself, that a Yankee fan will never understand.

But somehow I think, throughout those much too few, front porch summers, he knew. And he wanted me to know too.

And that's why I'm a Met fan.

I'm not ashamed to say it.

I'm a Met fan!

Smart Dog

Everyone thinks they have the smartest dog in the world.

They see them, sitting in front of the window for hours on end, surveying the neighborhood. You assume they're enjoying the goings on as their squirrel friends' frolic and their bird buddies skip from here to there.

Ahhhhh...what an idyllic life, to be a dog.

But maybe—just maybe—what your dog is really thinking is....

Where the heck am I, and how did I get here again?

Can I climb trees like that?

Is there any food?

But I guess a lot of you think I'm being too harsh and not giving the dog enough credit.

And I suppose you're right. At least the dog has enough sense to know, even though it's transparent, he can't walk through a glass door.

I've had party guests who don't know that, much to their chagrin and the door's.

The beauty of being a dog, or any animal, for that matter is it's a very instinctive, very intuitive being. It doesn't give a lot of thought to things...it just does things.

When it's hungry it eats. When it's sleepy it sleeps and when it's happy it licks your face...much like my old college roommate, whose records are still sealed.

On the other hand, we—the thinkers and analyzers of the world—can't do anything without picking it apart.

"I wonder how much fiber is in that cupcake?"

A dog sniffs the cupcake...eats the cupcake...takes a nap.

We walk by a mirror and think...*my ass is huge....*

A dog walks by a mirror and thinks...there's that hairy thing again...

We get invited out and think...*do I really feel like going out...is it raining...is it cold... do I want Italian or Chinese?*

A dog gets invited out, at any time, in any weather, and thinks...*ahhhhhhhh...that's better. Is there anything to eat?*

If your boss asks you to take a seat, you, think...*uh oh... what's this about?*

If you tell your dog to **"Sit"**, it thinks...*why does my butt always go down like that for no reason?*

"Roll Over"—*now that's weird.*

"Beg"—*what am I doing!*

And when you're done putting your dog through its paces....

I wonder if there's any food?

While you're worrying how you're gonna pay that Visa bill next month...

Did I really need those $200 Nikes?

Are these pants too tight?

We're so focused inward we miss that moment of pure Zen that is our dog...or cat...or gerbil.

Well, maybe not the gerbil, cuz who can tell what a gerbil is thinking.

Then by the time we snap out of it, the dog is sitting by the window again, one eye closing with sleep, a chew toy by its side.

Quite the life, we finally recognize, with not a little envy.

And the dog gives in, closes the remaining opened eye and thinks...

Where the heck am I, and how did I get here again?

Tomorrow

When I was a kid, "*tomorrow*" was a very vague and

flexible concept.

Tomorrow was when I would mow the lawn, write that English paper, throw away all those empty cartons of left over Chinese food that had accumulated under my bed throughout the months of January and February...okay, and sometimes March...and April.

There was always *tomorrow*.

I mean not that there isn't any more. Hopefully, at the tender age of 57, there're lots of tomorrows ahead for this Buckeroo...hopefully.

But let's face it, I'm at the age where the yesterdays are beginning to outnumber the tomorrows.

Right?

Just a bit....

Right?

Maybe....

It's always been hard to argue with yesterday.

That book's already been written...and yeah, maybe you did look a bit like the great unwashed and badly mustachioed during your college days; still, you were working it.

But there's no running away from those shirts with collars the size of Philadelphia you wore in your mid 20's.

And need I mention that squirrelly little pony tail you developed when you turned 40....

But not so tomorrow; tomorrow's an untold story full of fresh pages, rife with endless possibilities.

Once, tomorrow was when you'd worry about the results of all the errant behaviors you engaged in throughout your *"not now"* youth.

Things like cracking your knuckles.

"You're going to pay for that someday when you get arthritis fingers...."

"I'll worry about it tomorrow...."

Crack...!

Eating bowl after bowl of Hersey's chocolate syrup with 6 scoops of coffee ice-cream drowning somewhere underneath.

"Do you know what you're doing to your cholesterol...?"

"I'll worry about it tomorrow...."

Noshing on box after box of Oreos, Mallomars and Fig Newtons, just cuz you like em...you're darn tootin ...and on and on and on.

"You're gonna be so fat someday...."

"I'll worry about it tomorrow...."

When I was a kid I thought I was indestructible. I would bounce instead of break.

I wanted to be a stunt man so I would ride my bike through the park and fall off as if I was *shot by invisible enemy agents.*

No wall was too high for me to escape my wanna be captors.

I had the secret code that would disarm the dooms day device. I had to get it to the President!
Somebody had to....

There was no baseball, basketball or football too far to dive for...*not when there was a world championship at stake.*

My motto when playing sports was, *"If ya ain't dirty, you weren't trying hard enough".*

I even managed to get dirty playing tennis.

I used to fall over the net...*a lot.*

Somebody had to....

Whatever it was, the consequences didn't seem to apply at the time.

I'd worry about it tomorrow.

Well, now it's pretty much tomorrow and while I'm still not all that worried about it, I have to admit that various body parts and joints have been known to rise up and say... *"Ah haaaa!"* from time to time.

There are a couple of troublesome discs residing in my spine, both upper and lower regions that have been known on occasion to shout out, 'Hey, not so fast there ,buddy".

And my hands have been known to bark at me for about a week after hammering a couple of nails on a weekend...or folding my socks.

My back has been known to seize up on occasion; you know when I'm exerting myself...picking up the newspaper.

But for the most part so far so good.

My teeth are still intact...and more importantly still my own. But I need to make a dentist appointment.

Tomorrow....

My cholesterol and blood pressure seem to be okay, but I haven't seen a doctor to have it checked in about 15 years.

Tomorrow....

I walk 4, sometimes 8 miles a day... unless my knees are sending me nasty postcards reminding me of those 10 foot leaps, not to mention all those pavement pounding miles I accumulated during my 25 years of running.

I should probably see someone about that.

Tomorrow....

But right now I'm off for maybe my final trip to the beach this year before that aforementioned winter freeze sets in. My quickly fading summer skin is in dire need of a tune up.

I know...after 50 plus years of fun in the sun I should probably get a dermatologist to check me out.

And I will....

You know when....

Because it's always a day away.....

Cockeyed Optimist

To those who know me best, I'm sure this statement will elicit many snickers and tongue bites throughout the land.

But, still...I'm gonna say it....

I' m definitely not a pessimist.

Okay...now that you've got it out of your system, settle down and let me explain.

I'm really a cockeyed optimist...a *glass half full* kind of guy...but one who mostly sits around bemoaning the fact that, of course, now the ice cubes have melted.

So there's a distinction.

Sure, my Alpha-Bits cereal regularly forms words like *Woe, Doom and Pestilence*, which when you think of it is really quite a feat—a *positive* feat—but I'm usually able to look past that and maintain a cheery outlook. Something along the lines of, *chances are I probably won't get hit by a bus today.*

So that's positive....

In a cockeyed optimist kind of way.

Right...?

And I'm pretty sure I won't find something odd swimming in the bottom of my soup...not two days in a row.

Yet I have to admit, as I've said before, I'm prone to procrastination.

But I only procrastinate because I'm hoping to put off the inevitable that's inherent in whatever it is I'm procrastinating about.

It's been suggested I submit some of these witty works of Art— whom I'm annoyed with because Art hasn't shown up in a while— to assorted periodicals with the hope of actually making a few bucks out of it.

In fact I actually sat down to do that now...but instead I'm doing this.

Mostly cuz I like to save my rejection and disappointment for the holidays.

I put off getting a haircut for 6 months because I'm certain it's going to make me look like a dweeb.

Bingo!

I put off getting my oil changed because I expect they're going to find out my engine is single handedly destroying the ozone layer.

Bullseye!

I put off going to the dentist because I know he'll discover that my teeth have an expiration date that expired 5 years ago.

Ka-ching!

So I'm just trying to avoid all that because to be honest, who wants to spoil a perfectly good day? At least not until it's time.

You know...?

All positive.

We bought one of those "*assembly required*" desks from an unnamed Swedish furniture store a while back. Believe me, you can't shop at a place like that and be a pessimist.

Of course, I expected the drawer knobs and half the special hardware to be missing, so I wasn't at all surprised, let alone upset.

Besides the special Allen wrench needed to tighten the missing hardware that attached the missing drawer knobs was missing as well—also expected—so it all worked out for the best. And now it's easier to get to all my stuff since it's sitting in a pile on the floor, and not stuck in the back of some drawer.

Really, who needs that.....?

I spent 90 dollars on grass seed, but I wasn't expecting any of it to grow, mostly because I knew we would have a heat wave, it wouldn't rain for a month and I would put off watering it because I knew the nozzle on my hose was going to break.

So that wasn't at all disappointing.

And just because I buy lottery tickets and leave the store before they're printed doesn't mean I'm sure I won't win.

It only means I'm sure I'm gonna lose.

Another difference.

A positive difference.

An acceptance of the inevitable.

In fact it's what I was hoping for all along.

See...all healthy thinking!

So you see, it's really just a matter of attitude and outlook. I'm not a pessimist at all.

Just a cockeyed optimist who accepts his fate for what it is and knows it could be worse...and soon it probably will.

Just because the light you see at the end of the tunnel always turns out to be a train, doesn't mean you shouldn't hope for the best.

It only means you should avoid train tunnels.

And hope the train is the local and not the express....but it probably is.

What else would you expect?

They Clean Carpets

It's less than a couple of weeks 'til Thanksgiving and so we

did what just about everyone does just before the holiday fun begins...we had our carpets cleaned.

What...you don't?

Anyway, keeping with the holiday tradition, the carpet cleaners came the other day; a day I dread....

We hire them every year or so to come and steam clean the rugs, which they do, and do a nice job.

But I just can't stand their sense of righteousness. Not to mention the judgment....

"You want the stain guard treatment. right?"

"No...just the carpets, thanks."

"Mmmmm hmmmm. The upholstery?"

"Nope...just the carpets."

"How about your tile grout?"

"My tile grout is fine...thanks...again."

"You really don't want the stain guard treatment for only another $25.99?"

"No...just a cleaning, please"

"You're sure?"

"Positive..."

"It's not worth $25.99 knowing that you'll be free from worry in your high traffic areas...not to mention serious spill damage?"

"Pretty sure...."

"Pretty sure?"

Now I start to waver.

"I think."

"Think?"

But I recover. "Look, just clean the carpets. Okay?"

"Sure thing."

And with that one guy drags this huge hose through my living room while the other walks around looking for spots to spray with this magic super spot remover.

"So what's this...Merlot?"

"Could be...not really sure. How did you even see that?"

It was about the size of half a dime...under the couch.

"We're trained, sir. You throw a lot of parties?"

"Not a lot...some."

Then he's down on his hands and knees like a CSI investigator rubbing and sniffing. I start to feel like I need to fill in some of the gaps and offer, "I think it's from last Christmas."

"Christmas?"

"Yeah, we had Chicken." For some reason I thought that might be useful information.

"Chicken...for Christmas?"

"Yep...?"

"Most people have turkey."

"We had chicken". Now I'm beginning to feel a little ashamed.

"And you had red...with chicken?"

"Look, can you just clean the carpets, please."

"Yes, sir...we clean carpets...that's what we're here for."

And with that I head upstairs to escape the ridicule, but not before hearing the carpet investigator say to his partner, "I've got to get the kit out of the truck."

And while I'm no longer in the room, I can clearly see, at least in my head, the other guy shaking his head with disdain.

I really don't want to know what the kit is.

Soon there's all sorts of noise as the big machine is turned on, followed by the occasional chuckle, at least I think there's chuckles.

I peek down the stairs and spy the pair wearing these kind of plastic booties over their shoes, like the real CSI guys do, moving furniture and sucking up grime.

I start to head down the stairs, pleased to notice that the Merlot is a thing of the past.

"Whoa...hold on right there!" the man with the water sucker shouts. "Where do you think you're going with those dirty shoes?"

"Uh...nowhere?"

"No dirty shoes until this dries out for a day."

"Do you think I could have a pair of those booties then?"

Now I was using the word booties in a conversation that I was not at all enjoying. Plus the reaction I received was as if I had asked if I could drive their truck...blindfolded...while naked.

"Well, we're not really supposed to give out any booties."

I never knew a man could be so protective of his booties.

"Well, I'll be happy to pay extra for them," I offered.

The men looked at each other and shrugged. Apparently they had never been solicited for their booties before.

"Listen, if it's a problem I'll just walk in my socks. Don't worry about it."

"No...I'll give you some booties."

And now, as he reluctantly handed me the booties, I felt as if he thought my socks weren't good enough either. I put them on and began to inspect the work, feeling a little silly.

I noticed little squares of plastic under various chair legs and such and some blocks of foam under others. I recalled they were to protect the wet carpet from picking up any stain off the furniture legs. I wanted to impress the guys so I threw that little fact out there.

"Mmmmm hmmmm," was the best I could get out of them as they worked up my bill.

"It looks great!" I said, hoping to get some sort of a response.

"How old is this carpet?"

Here it comes, I thought, *the ax was about to fall.*

"5 years...four?"

"Uh...actually it's just 10. We bought it when we moved in."

"It's in really good shape, boss. You take nice care of it. I like people who take care of their carpets."

My chest swelled with pride as he handed me the receipt.

"Thanks...thanks," it was all I could utter, so shocked was I by this unexpected approval.

"You really should get the stain protector next time. You got lucky with that merlot."

"I'll think about it...promise. And thanks for the booties!"

With that I closed the door behind and swore I would not use the word booties again...at least for another year.

Ghoul Trouble

So now all the Zombies are mad at me, again.

Me....

Great!

Just what I need on Halloween...angry ghouls bad mouthing me on Twitter.

I mean what did I do?

I just introduced the Teenage Boy Zombie to the Teenage Girl Vampire, so now I'm the bad guy because someone said they're dating.

I mean one date is not a relationship.

It was just a movie and some ice cream afterward.

Sure...the Teenage Boy Zombie promised her his heart, but that was just the after effects of the Rom-Com talking.

Besides, he doesn't even know where his heart is anymore....

And yes... Teenage Girl Vampire did show a little too much fang...especially for a first date...but that sugar cone was pretty stale.

How else was she supposed to bite into it?

So now I have to deal with BOTH Zombie Dad AND Vampire Dad banging on my front door in the middle of the night.

I mean you know what it's like to be woken up by one angry ghoul?

Well, just double that.

Yeah....

And I'm innocent I tell ya....innocent.

The other day I was outside watching the Zombies put up their spook house, when Natalie—that's the Teenage Girl Vampire's name—walks over and asks me if we enjoyed the blood brownies she brought by the house the other day.

Naturally, I said we did, but you can guess where that whole tin ended up.

Anyway, who should shuffle over but Todd—the Teenage Boy Zombie—who starts flirting...you know, just a little flirting, in that Zombie way.

Showing off his muscles...or somebody's muscles...rolling his eyes at something funny Natalie said.

So what if he was rolling them down the driveway?

And that's when I walked off and left the two of them alone.

And apparently that was my BIG mistake.

Teenage Boy Zombies and Teenage Girl Vampires are never supposed to be left un-chaperoned.

Something cultural, I suppose.

Ghouls are very protective when it comes to bloodlines...both theirs and ours...if you catch my drift. And I guess it makes some sense.

Could you imagine a Vampire/Zombie Baby?

There's no telling what havoc *that* kid would reap.

So they try very hard to stick with their own kind.

And now they're saying I messed all that up.

But like I said...it was just one date.

Maybe a creepy date...but what do you expect from two spirited, undead teenagers?

I didn't know I was tainting the whole ghoulish gene pool.

Besides, I could tell right from the start that Natalie found Todd to be a little showy...you know with all the personal dismemberment.

At least now I hear they're breaking up...or at least Todd is...which is not all that unusual for a Zombie.

And Natalie is walking around as if someone pounded a stake through her heart...again...saying Todd was just an empty vessel of a man, anyway.

Ouch!

But that's how life is, I guess.

Even if technically, you're not really alive.

Love hurts...especially for those who walk the night.

What can I say....?

Gotta go get more Halloween candy.

Somehow the first 100 bags disappeared.

Weird....

Brian Moloney

The Circle of Leaves

Looking out the upstairs window, I see the last of the big

silver maple's somber melody of leaves falling to the lawn below.

An expected rite of passage for a leaf, at least from my stand point...not so much the leaf's.

Somewhere in the back of my head the theme from the Lion King plays as the circle of life unfolds. That and the theme from Mission Impossible, which I can't seem to shake either.

I first came upon them when they were just buds in January's eye, these leaves. Saw them begin to sprout in a sea of spring green, come April, until finally, fully blossomed in May, they sprang from branches and boughs, filtering the morning sun shining through this very same window.

Now the trees prepare for the long cold winter ahead and strip themselves bare. The leaves fall to the ground, decay and provide nutrients on which the tree will feed. That is until the army of leaf blower guys show up and screw up the whole Hakuna Matata thing.

Over the summer months I become very close with the leaves outside my window. I name them and everything.

What...you don't?

There's Burt and Lou. Melanie, Sarah, Todd...and Dave, who had that little fungus issue around August.

Bea, who's a little stuck on Lou. Lenny and Roxanne, who became a couple, with four off shoots of their own, two from previous hybrid arrangements.

Much too many to list here, but rest assured, all noted and appreciated throughout their too short season.

Of course we lost a lot of good leaves before their time this year with the hurricane in late August. They held on valiantly, but were overpowered by 50 mile an hour wind and rain.

They never had a chance to see their Chlorophylls degrade into colorless tetrapyrroles or experience their hidden pigments of yellow xanthophylls and orange beta-carotene revealed.

How cruel it seems sometimes, to live... to osmosify.

And now, even those most fortunate among leaves who refused to fly before their time, succumb to their natural cycle.

There goes Burt, now; he floats gracefully on the breeze as only Burt could...as only Burt would.

Melanie...blows a kiss as she settles on a bed of grass, still moist with morning dew.

Dave, always the complainer; bemoaning the fact that he only just began to feel like himself again...and now this.

Sarah...ah, sweet, sweet Sarah, so kind and understanding when I went through that little rough patch back in July; always the lady, at peace with her fate, happy to nurture the tree, from which she sprang.

Lou, the happy go lucky, yet stubborn one, who would have spit in the eye of the hurricane if he had lips; who would have brushed off the October snow, if he had arms...or a brush. Lou...still hanging on, feeling somehow he can make it through the winter, against all odds. Determined to be there come spring to welcome the new growth, to show them how it's done.

Ah...Lou...a true leaf among leaves. The lies we tell ourselves are the cruelest lies of all.

And though I'm sad to see these, my photosynthesized, foliated friends—so much more to me than than just the dense network of xylem and phloem you see them as—go gently into that good ...uhm...leaf sucker, I am heartened by the message of hope that they impart to me:

"We'll be back...as buds by mid-winter and sprouts in the spring...we'll be back. In every new leaf in every new season...we'll be there."

I'll keep an eye out for you my friends. There will always be a place for you here....It's the circle of leaves....

Man... that Mission Impossible theme is annoying....

Road Maps to the Past

Every now and then, while digging through the attic for my long lost pet rock collection, I come across an old Thanksgiving photo from the 60's.

It's often a group shot of my extended family sitting around a festive holiday table filled with food or, more likely, the remnants of food.

All familiar faces, minus the shadows of time; many now gone, but all still remembered.

These black and white road maps to my past are now the treasures of my present; opening doors to earlier days of innocence, wrapped in joy, sprinkled with pain...now embossed with smiles, knowing resolution always lingered just around the corner.

Little did we know, back then, when whoever grabbed that old Brownie Instamatic or Polaroid Swinger that we were actually staring into the future? That we were destined to be a moment frozen for all time; a moment left for future generations to ponder...or toss in the trash while cleaning out our attics.

That's the funny thing about old photos.

Prize to me...clutter to someone else.

The thing is, unless you were there, that captured moment is lacking something critical; something which can only be restored through our imaginations.

Noise!

What's lacking is the noise...the hub bub, the din...even the sound of my grandfather snoring, just off the right of picture frame.

Especially the sound of my grandfather snoring, just off the right of picture frame.

And with the clatter from the past restored in our minds, soon follows the colors, the smells, the textures and all the rest.

The laughter from the kitchen over who spilled the gravy. The arguments from the living room over what actually constitutes a fumble, both on TV and the front lawn...especially the front lawn.

The sight of your uncle—or somebody's uncle, of whom you were never quite sure—enlisting the drumsticks as ear decorations, which he did...every year...something he thought we wanted to see...every year.

The smell of meatball soup filling the room; too hot for some...too cold for others...still, always anticipated and always delicious.

Cranberry, in the shape of a can, wiggling on a small plate in the shape of a turkey, beckoning to all of us, shape notwithstanding, to be the first to deface its jellied perfection.

Fascination, as Grandma scoops out stuffing from a turkey's unmentionable nether region—*are we really gonna eat that stuff*—Gramps sharpening the BIG knife, all the while hatching a plan to keep the drumsticks away from the previously mentioned big eared mysterious uncle.

The pumpkin pie dropped, then zipped away and haphazardly reconfigured into semi-perfect slices, enlisting the five second rule as to why it was still mostly okay to eat...especially with cool whip...especially on Thanksgiving.

More laughter....more arguments...more of everything, packaged in black and white and sent off to the future.

Today, the memories come wrapped in digits of zeros and ones, very often already filled with sound and even music embedded. Everything future generations will ever need to peer back into an electronically flawless past....except imagination.

But, even so, as you sit at the table in this season of runaway holiday trains, pose by the turkey or sit by the tree, staring into your own future unknown, imagine that moment frozen in black and white, curled at the edges, preserving a lifetime of memories for you and everyone yet to come.

Just another thing to be thankful for.

Road Maps to the past.

Treasures of the present.

Even the guy with the drumsticks for ears....

A Hometown Christmas Story

Back in the mid 60's, when my friends and I were in the

6th grade, one of *our* favorite Hometown holiday traditions was to head on over to the new Shopping Center and play our version of *"The Man from U.N.C.L.E."* behind the pile of Christmas Trees they were selling.

The "tree guys" used to set up in the northeast corner of the parking lot. There, we would casually walk along the adjacent street in our coolest Napoleon Solo/Illya Kuryakin style, then suddenly drop over the guard rail and roll down the hill and into the mountain of trees, which kind of formed a hidden fortress on three sides.

We called our adventure the *"Yuletide Affair"* and day after day we would jump around in bales of evergreen, undetected by the "tree guys", or so we thought, until one day the delivery truck arrived and tree after Merry Christmas Tree came raining down on us from above.

Luckily, we were well trained agents and escaped to skulk another day; mostly against our friend Artie and his younger brother, Donnie, both of whom were unaware they were even being skulked.

I'm not sure why we did this; mostly because we were 11 with time on our hands, my friend Abner lived up the street and we liked humming the song.

All good reasons....

Okay...so it's not much of a Hometown Christmas story, but it's my Hometown Christmas story...lame or not.

See, that's the problem with writing a Hometown Christmas story. Everybody has one, and I know most of them are probably better than mine and go a lot further back.

Some of you grew up in the 20's, 30's and 40's or even a time before; a time that still buzzes inside you with life, rich with the detail of texture and color. To my mid to late baby boom generation, the 20's, 30's and 40's, like most things that came before us, are just mysteries wrapped in a collection of sepia toned photographs. The sights, the sounds, the feel of 1935 Main Street...I can't even begin to imagine.

Oh, sure, I've got some more stories, but the best I can offer is something like our catholic grammar school Christmas pageant, where the big highlight every year was the 8th graders standing as still as statues, recreating the Nativity scene. For some reason this was a big deal and always drew lots of applause, which is still a mystery to me since there wasn't an enemy agent to be found, let alone a cool theme song to hum.

So, I'm struggling here, rolling back to numerous Christmas Eves spent with my Italian and Irish grandparents, respectively, trying to dig up a good one—like, maybe the time my cousin blew linguini out of her nose when she found out what scungilli really was.

So there's that.

But the more I think about it, I guess I would have to say my most enduring Hometown Christmas memory would be that one night a year I traveled into our little village with my dad, to buy my mom's Christmas presents.

It would always be the last Thursday night, just before the big day. He'd walk into the house, right from the train, still carrying the chill of December on his long winter coat. The rest was routine: drop the keys on the side table, take off his hat, stick his brief case in the corner...except on this one night, there came the long awaited announcement...*"The men" are going shopping tonight!"*

A quick change of clothes followed, transferring pockets of jingling change from suit pants to khakis. Then, keeping to schedule, he'd pack me into our Black & White 57 Chevy—where the heat almost never worked, which accounted for the December chill thing—and off we went.

Our first stop was a cool little silver clad bakery I believe was called Topper's.

Topper's was the home of the world's greatest ginger bread men, or at least I thought so, and I suppose the idea was to provide me with something I could dismember, limb by limb, which would help keep me occupied...not to mention quiet on our long journey into the retail wilderness.

Now, I'm not sure why—maybe because it was such a rare occasion—but as we drove under the railroad bridge, Main Street was suddenly alive with magic; an endless tunnel of colorful lights and garland, dancing from every light pole, across one side of the street to the other.

A Christmas tree, which to a 6 year old was as big as the one in Rockefeller Center, lit up the Village Square, and the sound of bells ringing from strategically placed Santas created a cacophonous effect, accompanying the buzz and bustle of shoppers crowding the sidewalks as far as my eyes could see.

Of course, I would like to say it was snowing, and maybe it was, at least once—I'm not sure—but it was *always* frosty and my nose would run as we rambled in and out of creaky storefront doors. However, unlike my mom, who was always at the ready—and the nose—with a tissue, my dad would just say *"wipe that runny thing"*, which left the how to my own ingenuity, which I won't get into at this time.

On it went, from one store to the other we'd wander in search of *"mom"* gifts; and the thing that was most amazing, at least to me, was how nice all the sales ladies were to my dad, in a way that they were never *"as nice"* to my mom. There were always lots of smiles, giggles and even a few wiggles, as he had a way of making all of them, even the sternest ladies from the dreaded Kaplan's, laugh at his feigned helplessness, while they produced the latest in early 60's fashion for our perusal.

A poofy hat with a weird kind of netting and possibly a feather.

A fuzzy sweater with strange little beads and maybe a poodle stitched on the pocket.

My dad would hold up each item, looking this way and that, then finally turn to me and say, *"Which one do you think?"*

I would study each item carefully, then point to the one that had the most blue in it, pretty much the same as I still do today.

Afterwards, with a job well done, we would stop at the local soda shop for a hot chocolate and a—

Well, in the official Frank Capra and mom version that's how it might have gone. But in reality it was more like the local downtown tavern for a slice of pizza and a *"Pop for Pop"* as he might have said it.

Then the short ride home, where I always fell asleep, and it always snowed in my dream.

So, I guess that's it...my hometown Christmas story...and I wouldn't write it any other way.

You from the Outside...Looking In

If you're a lot like me...well, then I feel bad for you.

And stop being so annoying!

No...that's not what I meant...but really...*STOP!!!*

Sorry...

What I meant to say was, if you're a lot like me....

Okay...I've got this, now....

If you're a lot like me, then you pretty much think absolutely no one in the world really knows you like you know you.

How could they?

How could they know you secretly enjoy watching and collecting Britney Spears music videos from the late 90's.

Or that you still keep an 8 track tape player hidden in your glove compartment, just so you can listen to all your old ABBA tapes from the 70's.

All defining characteristics as to who I...I mean *you*...really are.

Well, that and the public records that had, until recently, been sealed.

I mean who knew it was illegal to drink a Budweiser in Boston? Seriously...who?

But secret choices of music or beer isn't really what I'm talking about.

I'm talking about the difference in how we see ourselves compared to the way in which the rest of the world sees us...even our closest and most enduring friends...including the 3,600 friends you have on Facebook.

Many of us walk around every day with a constant narration running through our brains.

I don't mean like secrets messages from your hamster telling you that you need to straighten out Pat, with the Poodle cut, who constantly helps herself to the diet coke you stash in the back of the break room fridge, every day.

I mean more benign things, like:

I have to polish these shoes sometime before the next decade.

Or, I really like how I look in red, but do people think I'm just showing off?

I think that new girl in accounting really likes me...but maybe she's just staring at my mole.

The neighbors must think I'm odd because I like to sit in the attic and stare out the window all day on Saturday and Sundays.

Hey, it's the weekend...what else am I...I mean are *you*...supposed to do?

We only see ourselves from the inside looking out, with our friend, the narrator, constantly keeping tabs.

Constantly telling us how the rest of the world, on the outside looking in, sees us.

Or so we think...or more accurate, so the narrator thinks.

And how many times has the narrator held us back from things we really want to do in our lives?

I can't audition for Dancing with the Stars...not after the incident at the Kirby's wedding....

My rendition of "Oklahoma" is flawless but there's no way I'm getting up at Karaoke night... not until they get rid of that Sushi Chef who looks at me funny.

I should really submit my proposal to incorporate personal robots into the traffic department, but maybe not until the boss stops thinking I'm the UPS guy.

True or not true...I don't know? But that's the kind of thing we tell ourselves, every time we want to take a chance with something.

Even worse, it's very often the kind of things the narrator tell us to think twice about, even when we're really not taking a chance at all.

Little things like deciding to write a poem and showing it to our friends.

Picking up a guitar and strumming it at a party.

Making a toast at your best friend's wedding.

Making a presentation in front of your peers.

Creating art in stained glass or concrete mushrooms.

All the things that, much too often, we see from the inside, looking out through the skewed windows attached to our minds.

They're all looking at me like I'm odd.

They think I should stick to playing my iPod.

That guy over there is looking at me weird.

That woman in the corner is trying hard not to laugh at me.

But the reality is, from the outside looking in, all those people are really saying is...

Hey, I wish I could put myself out there like that.

That was such a beautiful poem.

She gave such a beautiful toast.

I wish my mushrooms were as nice as that....

Hmmm...I wonder if the effects I feel from that chili dog are making me look weird...and is that woman in the corner laughing at me...again?

So who would you say really knows you best: you...looking from the subjective inside out...or everybody else...looking from the objective outside in?

You against everybody else... everybody else against you...and the narrator?

Maybe we should just go with the odds.

But you're probably thinking this is the dumbest idea you ever heard.

I can actually hear the sneering.

Maybe I shouldn't even post this...it's really kind of out there.

Oops...I just hit the post button.

How do I retract....how do I retract...?

I can't find the delete button....

I didn't really mean to put this out there....

This is really embarrassing....

Acknowledgment

Thanks to all the Retorters who have been with me on this ride from the beginning. Your support and, of course, pithy comments are always appreciated. On those low occasions when that annoying voice in my head says, *"Why the heck are you doing this, when you could be spending your time more wisely, organizing your old comic book collection?"* I pause and remember...it's for you...that's the heck.

And if you're new to the Retorts, where the heck have you been? Welcome to the club. Jump on-line and join us for all latest silliness. Your membership card and t-shirt is in the mail...somewhere...and don't forget to bring the cupcakes to the next meeting....

The Freelance Retort
Something to Laugh About...sometimes

freelanceretort.blogspot.com

About the Author

Brian Moloney (that's me) has worked in the communications fields of Advertising, Film and TV on both the commercial and corporate sides, since 1978. He (still me) began freelancing as a writer in 1992, when he discovered he could type on a computer without the need of whiteout to hide all his mistakes; a process he found extremely messy and time consuming. In addition to "The Zombies Have Big Heads" he's authored "The Kingdom of Keys", a Young Adult, Action/Adventure/Fantasy story and "The Little Red Christmas Ball", a story for kids and anyone whoever was...and would be again...available thru all major on-line booksellers. Currently, he's at work compiling a second volume of essays from "The Freelance Retort", which he threatens to finish and send out soon...very, very soon.

"The Freelance Retort" can be found on-line at freelanceretort.blogspot.com
And on Facebook, along with all the cats and everything else....
Email the Author: freelanceretort@gmail.com

Also Available thru Major On-line Booksellers

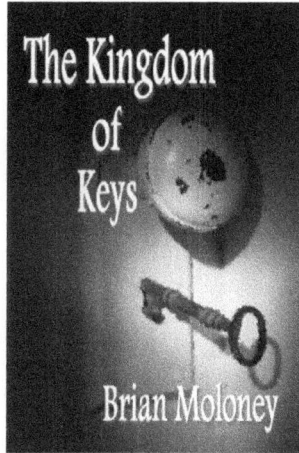

Sixteen year old Toby Pierce is lost, disillusioned and just not happy with the path his life has taken ever since circumstances, four years earlier, changed the course of *everything* he knew as normal. That is, until he discovered the key...*always the key*...to the mysterious *Door to Nowhere*, a perpetually locked, never used, sealed doorway, tucked in the corner of his room.

A strange prophetic dream leads Toby to confront the key and - with the semi-unflagging support of his two best friends, Lori and Billy–unlock the *Door to Nowhere*. An explosive reception soon follows as the trio is transported to the magical *Kingdom of Keys*, where Toby chooses to follow the path of the *Doors*. There, he struggles to learn the secret of the seed...the heart...the soul...the passion...the mind...and most of all, how really simple it all is...if we just have the faith to *allow it to be*....

Action, adventure, fantasy, humor, villains, heroes, Kings, Queens, strange creatures from an enchanted land and a multitude of laser blasts; these are the fundamental elements of *The Kingdom of Keys*. But, more importantly, woven within is an insightful message designed to encourage young minds to choose the path in life most in harmony with, not only their intellect, but also their heart and their soul.

Also Available thru Major On-line Booksellers

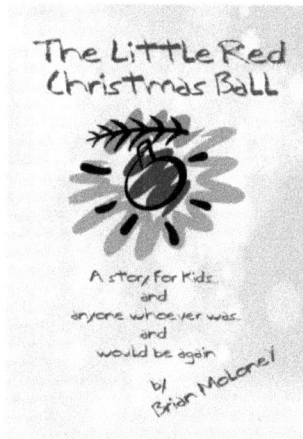

The Little Red
Christmas Ball

A story for kids
and
anyone who ever was
and
would be again
by
Brian McLane

Nestled within the confines of a modern day family, The Little Red Christmas Ball is the last of the colorful breed of vintage ornaments that, once upon a time, shined brightly from within and sparkled tirelessly among the trees of yesterday.

Passed down through the years, the Little Red Christmas Ball has become—these days—just a tad insecure as he finds himself more often than not relegated to the rear of the majestic Christmas tree. He fears he's become, well, just a little bit ordinary in this modern age of ornaments equipped with manufactured charm. Nonetheless, the Little Red Christmas Ball is secure in the knowledge—*he thinks*—his true purpose is to shine bright and provide good Christmas cheer.

Until one particular Christmas Eve the unthinkable occurs and the Little Red Christmas Ball is unknowingly knocked from his little evergreen home.

"What kind of a Little Red Christmas Ball would I be if I missed a Christmas? I would have no purpose, no purpose at all...."

Soon, with the help of three disparate, late-night housemates, the quest begins to return the Little Red Christmas Ball to his rightful place upon the Christmas Tree before Santa arrives.

www.ingramcontent.com/pod-product-compliance
Lightning Source LLC
Chambersburg PA
CBHW071533040426
42452CB00008B/1001